Getting It
Done

Project Management in Action

Stories from
PMNetwork®

ISBN: 978-1-62825-114-2

Published by: Project Management Institute, Inc.
                       14 Campus Boulevard
                       Newtown Square, Pennsylvania 19073-3299 USA
                       Phone: +610-356-4600
                       Fax: +610-356-4647
                       Email: customercare@pmi.org
                       Internet: www.PMI.org

PMI Publications welcomes corrections and comments on its books. Please feel free to send comments on typographical, formatting, or other errors. Simply make a copy of the relevant page of the book, mark the error, and send it to: Book Editor, PMI Publications, 14 Campus Boulevard, Newtown Square, PA 19073-3299 USA.

To inquire about discounts for resale or educational purposes, please contact the PMI Book Service Center.

                       PMI Book Service Center
                       P.O. Box 932683, Atlanta, GA 31193-2683 USA
                       Phone: 1-866-276-4764 (within the U.S. or
                       Canada) or +1-770-280-4129 (globally)
                       Fax: +1-770-280-4113
                       Email: info@bookorders.pmi.org

10 9 8 7 6 5 4 3 2 1

TABLE OF CONTENTS

PART 2: TECHNICAL PROJECT MANAGEMENT

PART 3: STRATEGIC AND BUSINESS MANAGEMENT

FOREWORD

Earlier in my career, I worked for an organization that found a great deal of success through "brute force management." This approach succeeded due to the many smart and dedicated people who worked very hard to get things done.

What we didn't have were standards, practices, frameworks or tools. We had no consistent approach to achieving outcomes. We did not capture and share lessons learned. And I wish I could say that we understood how our work contributed to overall organizational success. In truth, with every new project, we basically started over.

In retrospect, we "got it done," but we wasted resources and perhaps accomplished less than we might have if we had known about and embraced a formal project management approach.

Within these pages, you will find inspiring stories that vividly demonstrate the value of your profession. Written by project managers, each story in *Getting It Done: Project Management in Action* provides a real-life account of such project challenges as marshaling resources, battling waste, and managing stakeholders, business owners and competing priorities.

As a project manager, you might be managing risk in complexity, an infrastructure project, new product development or supervising completely virtual teams. Whatever challenges you face—and I know there are many—your colleagues around the world have experienced similar issues and found ways to manage them successfully.

Each story in this book has a particular purpose. Each was chosen to illustrate the importance of the three sides of the PMI Talent Triangle™: technical proficiency, leadership capability, and strategic business management skills.

I first sketched the talent triangle in 2010 as a visual to clarify what I was hearing from executives in organizations using project management—that technical project management skills, while very important, were no longer enough. These executives were saying, and continue to say, very clearly that project managers also need leadership skills, along with strategic and business insight in order to be successful. They have identified these capabilities as next-generation project manager

characteristics. They consider them indispensable to remaining relevant and viable in today's highly competitive global business environment. Our *Pulse* research shows that project managers are most successful when they have strong leadership skills. This applies both early in their careers and for the long term.

As you read these stories, you will find clear examples of the skill areas most sought by organizations in hiring and developing project management talent. One story tells how to break into the video game industry. You will also learn about the three requirements for a great agile team. You will read how one practitioner built a curriculum to teach a master's level university course in project management in Cameroon. You will discover lessons learned from a practitioner on a team involved with putting on the 2016 Olympics. You will even acquire career advice, including the three questions every project manager should be prepared to answer in a job interview.

I am confident that you will enjoy and learn from the experiences shared by your fellow project managers. And I hope they inspire you to share yours by contributing to the "Getting It Done: Project Management in Action" column in *PM Network®*.

Together, we can do great things.

Mark A. Langley
President and CEO
Project Management Institute

Part 1

Leadership

It seems to be common sense that the project manager who has to lead a team must have leadership skills. Yet, in many organizations, promotions to team leader or project manager sometimes go to people highly skilled in technical areas and somewhat lacking in leadership abilities.

Leadership skills, sometimes called "soft" or "people" skills, are absolutely essential in bringing projects to successful closure. This is especially the case when project team members cross generations, cultures, nationalities, languages and time zones. Other skills covered by this side of the PMI Talent Triangle include negotiation, communication, motivation and problem solving.

On the following pages are columns covering some of the most common people-related issues you might come across in your own projects. These challenges include conveying bad news to your client or sponsor, making meetings productive and taking care of your team.

The articles in this section provide methods and tips that you might not expect. For example, did you know that you can use video games to teach collaboration and even emotional intelligence? You will learn how to use a 10-minute meeting to improve project team communication, divert a team member with an outsized ego by assigning him or her a lead role on a side activity communicating to a limited set of stakeholders, and use emotional detachment to better solve project problems.

Learning the Hard Way

Spend time building your team—
or risk poor performance.

Mário Henrique Trentim, PMI-RMP, PMP, PfMP

Project success generally depends on whether stakeholders are happy with a project's results. On each project, we do our best to get stakeholders involved, collect the right requirements, and manage expectations for stakeholders, sponsors and clients.

So why do our projects get in trouble during execution? I believe it's because we focus on trying to please clients and sponsors, and keeping the project on track—and we forget to take care of the team.

We can't manage people in the same way we manage cash, schedule and resources. We have to lead them. Happy team members work better and faster. If you spend time building your team, you'll get better performance. Here's how:

- **Keep team members informed.** The project team should know what to do, how to do it and when to do it. But above all, they have to know why they are

doing it. When a project manager can show each team member how his or her work supports the project objectives, there is a sense of responsibility, accountability and ownership for the team member. When the team is aware of consequences and trade-offs, it will be more proactive.

We focus on trying to please clients and sponsors, and keeping the project on track—and we forget to take care of the team.

- **Get to know team members.** As project managers, we have to guide our teams and earn their trust. To do that, we have to take care of them, get to know them, and understand their feelings and expectations.

   This isn't always an easy task, and it takes time. Every person has his or her own quirks and characteristics, and you have to be interested in discovering them. Build open communication by having frequent one-on-one meetings to discuss issues, performance and motivators. Having lunches, happy hours and team activities also provides important moments of interaction between team members and the project manager.

- **Protect your team.** You must support and protect your project team members—they are your most valuable assets. Protect them from external interferences, so they can work in peace and do their best. You're responsible for your team members; you have the authority to assess them and give them feedback. If there is an issue, confront it. When you allow external people to give assignments or even reprimand your team members, you lose control and the team's trust.

  To avoid this, you, as the project manager, must be the focal point of the project. Every external stakeholder must talk to you, and all team members can only accept assignments from you.

> When you allow external people to give assignments or even reprimand your team members, you lose control and the team's trust.

- **Use positive reinforcement.** Think back to when you were a student or a trainee and how difficult it was in the beginning. Do you remember those who helped you along the way? A good project manager, just like a good teacher, has to understand the difficulties that their team members face. Positive

reinforcement leads to cooperation more than rewards and coercion do. Motivate your team members individually and as a group by celebrating their
breakthroughs and victories. Even little accomplish-
ments can be opportunities for praise.

Remember that as project managers, we are part of a
team—we are not above anyone. Your number-one role
is as team leader. Always try to create a positive environment, even when things are tough. If you focus on
the positive side of people, you likely will get their best.

Mário Henrique Trentim, PMI-RMP, PMP, PfMP, is the director of
research at the Brazilian Institute for Corporate Development -
IBADE, São Paulo, Brazil.

The Four P's

Four techniques for powering a failing project toward success.

Have you ever been handed a failing project or struggled to complete one? I once took over a project that was spiraling toward failure. It was behind schedule (little had been achieved since its inception six months earlier), the project team was not communicating or working together effectively, and there was no rapport between the previous project manager and the client. However, I was able to remedy the situation by applying the four "P" techniques that I'd used in previous projects.

1. PRODUCTIVE TEAM COMMUNICATION

Conducting regular status meetings and building a rapport with the project team are critical to achieving success. These meetings should be about more than reviewing the status of tasks—they're an opportunity to discuss challenges and risks. Multiple perspectives contribute to a more comprehensive product and can help resolve any problems that arise. To build team rapport,

I ask for a member to share a joke or funny story at the conclusion of every meeting. This levity is especially important when managing a virtual team: We may not be in the same room, but we can still have fun together. After the meeting, I distribute meeting minutes and action items, to ensure accountability and progress.

2. POSITIVE AND NEGATIVE CLIENT COMMUNICATION

No one likes to give a client bad news. But delivering both the good and the bad gives the project manager credibility with a client. Being direct and up front with a client about delays or problems leads to open and honest communication, which promotes a healthy and trusting relationship. It also gives the client the opportunity to provide a different perspective and identify solutions while addressing schedule delays, budget concerns or the resolution of risks. If there is bad news, project managers should frame it as an opportunity to assess what is going on, and then reset the client's expectations through a new plan. Don't deliver bad news empty-handed; offer options to your client and guide him or her to the most appropriate option.

3. PERSISTENCE

More often than not I'm nicknamed "Hound" while managing a project. While some might be offended by this, I claim the name as a badge of honor. Whether you're nudging your team members or your client, persistence pays off (though sometimes it takes longer than you'd like). The action item list that comes out of weekly status meetings, for example, is a good tool to hold your team or client accountable. Of course, reminders—whether delivered in person, via email or over the phone—are a go-to mechanism to prod people and encourage on-time delivery.

> Whether you're nudging your team members or your client, persistence pays off (though sometimes it takes longer than you'd like).

4. PASSION

If you exude passion, your team members are more likely to follow suit. Leading by example matters when managing projects: It is easier to emulate a passionate project manager than a disgruntled one. But be careful not to be emotional; always lead with a calming demeanor.

Turning around the troubled project I took over was undoubtedly a team effort, but these four "P" techniques enabled me to successfully lead the project across the finish line. The experience was a reminder of the techniques' effectiveness in difficult situations and also how valuable they've been to my career as a project manager. While I may not be able to quantify the value of these techniques, I can say with confidence that they've helped build my reputation as a project manager who can turn a challenging project into a success in any environment.

Yael Cohen, PMP, is a freelance program manager in Denver, Colorado, USA.

Go Team

Increasing efficiency makes for a more motivated team—and better project outcomes.

Deepa Gandhavalli Ramaniah, PMP

Consider the following stakeholders: customers, sponsors, team members and managers. Of those groups, which one do you think project managers consider the most important?

I believe team members are. From initiation to closure, the team helps the project managers run and deliver a successful project. Because of their day-to-day importance, making teams work more efficiently and effectively should be the top priority for project leaders.

Several best practices allow for improved efficiencies and enable project managers to help team members excel. Here, I have coined an acronym, "TEAM," comprised of the best practices for creating an efficient team.

TAILOR TO THE TEAM'S NEEDS
Tailoring to team members' needs, expectations and concerns helps ensure that project tasks get done and the team's expectations are met. To discover what

> **From initiation to closure, the team helps the project managers run and deliver a successful project. Because of their day-to-day importance, making teams work more efficiently and effectively should be the top priority for project leaders.**

your team's needs and expectations are, I suggest the following:

- During project initiation, meet with team members on a one-on-one basis to identify their goals. For example, a coder on an IT project might aspire to become a designer.
- Assign tasks based on their expectations, which should increase productivity and quality output. If conflicting needs from team members arise, project managers should use their negotiation skills to illustrate the reasons why the need cannot be fulfilled, and at the same time provide alternative solutions that still keep team members motivated.
- Get the activity resource estimates from team members during project planning and have them review the project plan to ensure that it is realistic.
- Conduct one-on-one meetings monthly to learn the team's concerns during project execution and address them immediately.
- Create a comfort zone through informal chats that help team members believe their issues will be addressed.

EMPOWER THE TEAM

How a project manager delegates tasks has a direct impact on the team members who affect the success of the project.

An efficient project manager cares not only about getting things done, but also about the project team's growth.

The conventional approach of delegating tasks includes giving a deadline and asking for frequent status updates on the schedule. I believe this pursuit creates a lot of work and stress, de-motivates team members and decreases quality output. Instead, empower the team to feel motivated to complete tasks on time with the following practices:

- Identify areas of improvement within the project and ask the team to come up with ideas, such as a change in systems development life-cycle processes or an introduction of latest technologies. This shows trust in your team.

- Subject-matter experts in each domain or module can assist the entire team by resolving issues in their area of specialty—and therefore reduce the team's workload.

- Promote innovation by setting appropriate yearly development goals for team members, in addition to their operational or performance goals. Take initiative in presenting innovative ideas to the team to show such thinking is encouraged.
- Initiate 360-degree feedback, which enables the team to give constructive advice and criticism about the project manager.

ANALYZE TEAM PROGRESS

Note that I say "team progress" and not "project progress." An efficient project manager cares not only about getting things done, but also about the project team's growth.

- Set clear goals and objectives for each individual based on his or her competence and career path.
- Analyze and provide guidance on how to achieve the team member's goals.
- Set up lessons-learned meetings to analyze what went well and what went wrong.

MOTIVATE THE TEAM

Constant motivation builds energy for the team atmosphere. I follow certain practices to create a motivated environment:

- Recognize and appreciate team members for their efforts, small or big. Provide continuous appreciation in meetings and email responses, and set up awards such as the "Monthly Power Performer" or "Best Innovator" for approved ideas.
- Conduct frequent team outings and team-building activities. For example, celebrate birthdays each month,

host a new joiners' induction program or attend weekly happy hours.

- Arrange training sessions.
- Encourage the use of the latest technologies, which drives the team to gain knowledge on new concepts and incorporate them into their project.

Deepa Gandhavalli Ramaniah, PMP, is senior associate—projects at Cognizant Technology Solutions, Chennai, India.

Alter the Ego

How to make team members with big personalities your allies.

Diane Haubner, CISA, PMP

On a recent six-month project to select a new electronic health record (EHR) system for a hospital, I led a team of technical experts, nurses, hospital administrators and physicians. Within these groups were a few egomaniacs who longed for control.

I understood their plight: They were thrust into roles that didn't mirror their day-to-day jobs where they felt comfortable.

But I didn't want a power struggle. I wanted allies. So I asked myself: When a project has a team member who feels the need to be on top, how can a project manager lead that large personality without bruising his or her ego and losing project support?

BEGIN WITH BABY STEPS

To start, communicate project processes, as these are often new to team members. You need to quickly build familiarity in a very unfamiliar world.

As soon as an infringement of one of the processes occurred, I noted it publicly in a weekly meeting without placing blame or referencing any one individual. I also recognized there was a learning curve. This showed all parties that the processes were being taken seriously and monitored earnestly.

CONTACT A HIGHER POWER

The project manager also needs to find an executive-level resource who can be trusted and relied upon for input and advice. This higher-up should already have a relationship with the individual and have the authority to assist when issues arise.

In my EHR project, I reached out to an executive who had experience with physicians. To lend more credibility to project processes, I asked him to speak publicly at physician meetings to state and re-state how project objectives benefited the hospital's overall success and, ultimately, individual healthcare success for practitioners and patients.

CREATE A SPLASH ZONE

Often, egomaniacs feel like big fish in a small pond. In my case, I let one team member splash on occasion without creating big, disruptive waves.

One way to do this is assigning the individual a lead role in a piece of communication to a particular audience. By keeping the person busy on a required—and public—activity, you satisfy attention-seeking egos without disrupting the project.

For example, one physician on my EHR project was paid to be the liaison between vendors and physician partners. He met regularly with other physicians in after-work sessions that included food and drinks—and kept his peers both updated on the project and happy.

SCHEDULE FACE TIME

Midway through the EHR project, I discovered that written updates about project activities were, by and large, ignored by stakeholders. The reason? They felt like their feedback on the project wasn't being heard.

I changed my communications method to generate more face-to-face feedback opportunities with the physicians at off-site locations. Given a comfortable, open environment, the physicians felt their opinions were heard and respected.

When a project has a team member who feels the need to be on top, how can a project manager lead that large personality without bruising his or her ego and losing project support?

BE NICE—AND GENUINE

The project manager must also privately and publicly commend individuals on good performance. To prompt even better performance, these compliments have to be sincere. Made-up flattery will get you nowhere, as the stakeholder is likely to see it as the mere ego-massage tactic it is.

Keeping big egos in check is a tall order, but done carefully and methodically, even me-first personalities can be team players.

Diane Haubner, CISA, PMP, is a senior project manager at Acacia Consulting, Milwaukee, Wisconsin, USA.

Talking Points

Lessons learned from public-speaking training can have universal application.

Peggy Pleasant, PMP

After participating in public-speaking training for more than a decade, I've learned numerous communications skills, including how to organize a speech and speak off the cuff.

But I've come to realize that the leadership lessons I've learned from public-speaking courses not only help me talk in front of crowds but also make me better at all aspects of my job.

SING PRAISES, NOT PROCESS

The speech workshops I've attended are extremely motivational. Participants are encouraged to support each other and applaud one another's efforts. My peers help me accomplish my speech goals, and vice versa.

Project managers should do the same for their teams. Like many project managers, I am responsible for the success or failure of a project, although I have no formal authority over my team members. Yet I still have to

move team members to follow processes that will help us reach our end goal. To do so, I motivate team members, instead of pushing process on them.

For example, I take advantage of my company's employee-recognition program by shooting a kudos email to a team member's manager. Then I pass that praise on to human resources so that the team member's good work makes it into the monthly company newsletter.

TALK ABOUT SOLUTIONS, NOT PROBLEMS
I've worked on projects with a variety of issues such as timeline concerns, scope creep and overbearing customers. To maneuver past these challenges, I've learned from

public-speaking training to focus my communication with team members on solutions rather than problems.

If the project is off schedule, I ask, "What steps can we take to adjust tasks and maintain the critical path?" as opposed to "How did we get so far off track?"

Such a communications tactic encourages a collaborative environment and eliminates any potential for a "woe is me" atmosphere.

SPEAK OF STRENGTHS FIRST, NOT WEAKNESSES

In my speech workshops, participants are encouraged to critique each speaker and provide a list of "glows" (things they did well in the speech) and "grows" (things they can improve).

Evaluation is just as important in project management. But while lessons learned are a must, giving feedback on a project that was less than flawless (is there such a thing as a perfect project?) can make team members uncomfortable. This process can be so distressing for the team that there's a tendency to quickly move on to the next project without discussing the project issues that can be improved for future efforts.

Again, the focus in my lessons learned meetings is on solutions, not problems. This eliminates stress and improves relationships and trust among team members.

While great project managers don't have to be great public speakers, the skills you learn to become the latter can increase the chances of project success.

Peggy Pleasant, PMP, is a business process consultant, City of Austin, Austin, Texas, USA.

Huddle Up

Tailor stand-up meetings to clear communication hurdles between program and project managers.

John Pitchko, PMP

Last year, our IT program delivery group noticed that traditional communication methods were no longer effective. Our weekly check-ins with project managers weren't frequent enough for project managers to raise issues promptly. We also noticed that program managers would forget about reported issues because we were not diligent in recording and regularly reviewing issues.

We needed more frequent meetings to help us resolve issues soon after they occurred—and before they escalated to critical importance. However, we needed a time-sensitive format that would help encourage people to sacrifice more time in their busy schedules and attend. If meetings were too long or too frequent, team members would not support them.

TAKING A STAND

The solution: the huddle concept, gleaned from lean principles. Traditionally, these 10-minute daily meetings require all participants to stand to ensure quick discussion.

But we made a few adaptations to fit our needs. We scheduled biweekly meetings consisting of all program and project managers. Our initial huddles were scheduled for 30 minutes, but this time has since been cut in half now that we are experienced at executing quick meetings.

During every huddle, each project manager in the program has two minutes to speak about his or her project and state whether any issues need escalation. For example, a project manager may report a sponsor is unresponsive to project requests, and a program manager can step in.

To help track these issues, we created a huddle board, a piece of laminated plotter paper posted on the wall of the meeting room. The visual representation allows program managers to easily see which projects require their attention first. It also gives us a starting point for each huddle: We review each escalation on the board, and tick off the resolved issues or develop new plans of action for those unresolved.

LEARNING TO TALK

We thought this custom huddle system would solve our communications woes. But our group encountered a few challenges after launching it.

Most team members are in the office each day, but a handful work at different locations, making it difficult for everyone to contribute to huddles. To address this problem, we opened a teleconference line at each meeting.

Still, virtual workers couldn't see the huddle board. So we are now investigating options to make a digital representation of our huddle board to share with remote workers.

Another challenge is shyness. Huddles are about communication, but more reserved members hesitate to speak up. Even the extroverts find the meetings' mission—to identify projects' pain points—difficult to talk about. They may be too proud or nervous to ask for help as they may see it as an admission of weakness.

We've learned the huddle is a powerful method for improving communication between program and project managers.

To help communication flow, we removed the red/green traffic light system of the typical project dashboard. We also do not use terminology such as "needs help," "red project" or "low confidence." Instead, we ask whether or not projects "need attention," which focuses the conversation on the actions required, not problems occurring.

BABY STEPS

Our huddle is still in its infancy, but we are starting to see benefits. When I've spoken with program managers about it, I've discovered they feel better able to track which projects need their involvement. We've learned the huddle is a powerful method for improving communication between program and project managers.

John Pitchko, PMP, is a program manager at oil and gas company Shell, Calgary, Alberta, Canada.

Ominous Silence

The five taboo topics that can doom projects.

David Maxfield

Project management requires frank, honest and respectful dialogue. But what if the problems you see with a plan, a sponsor or a team member feel too taboo to mention?

In these cases, information-based processes and tools are of little help. Solving "undiscussables" requires deeper changes to cultural practices, social norms and personal skills.

The corporate training firm VitalSmarts investigated more than 2,200 projects, looking for undiscussables, categorizing them and measuring their impact. We discovered that the vast majority of project failures involve five undiscussables.

1. **Fact-free planning.** About 85 percent of project participants in the survey reported project deadlines, budgets or resources being set without consideration for reality. Fewer than one in seven

practitioners were able to successfully confront the problem. When this crucial conversation fails, there is an 82 percent chance the project will come in over budget, late or short on quality.

2. **Absent sponsors.** The study found 65 percent of project managers experience sponsors who don't provide adequate leadership, political clout, time or energy. Furthermore, 88 percent of practitioners describe confronting this situation as between "difficult" and "impossible." Fewer than one in five are able to hold the crucial conversation in a way that solves the problem. When the project leader fails to solve this problem, more than three-quarters of projects come in substantially over budget, behind schedule and below specifications.

3. **Lack of planning.** The study found 83 percent of project leaders routinely contend with stakeholders who skirt the formal project planning process. This leads to scope creep, a problem that only 13 percent of respondents are able to resolve. As a result, 80 percent of these projects fail to achieve their deliverables.

4. **Inaccurate status reports.** Projects derail when team members fail to honestly report their status. More than half of project managers say they regularly face some form of this, and fewer than one in four are able to resolve it. When status reports are not reported honestly, 74 percent of these projects fall short of requirements.

5. **Team failures.** Eighty percent of project leaders report being hobbled by team members who don't attend meetings, fail to meet schedules or lack the competence to meet ambitious goals. Often these

leaders have little say in selecting or replacing these non-performers and feel powerless to coach them. Instead, they ignore their deficiencies and work around the problem. The study showed that when project managers fail to effectively address performance problems in their teams, four out of five projects suffer from budget, schedule and quality problems.

WHAT PROJECT MANAGERS CAN DO

Some project managers are able to successfully resolve these problems, even in unwelcoming environments. Here's how:

Recognize what must be said. Project managers who see the danger in their projects are more likely to speak up.

Hold the right conversation. When you don't address exactly what's wrong, you leave the real problem unsolved. For example, a project manager might approach an absent sponsor and say, "We missed you at the last meeting." This is the wrong conversation. The problem is not so much the recent absence, but the pattern of missed commitments.

Lead with facts. Skillful project managers lay out the factual basis of their concerns before sharing the riskier conclusions. For example, "Our Asia office is now six months behind in getting us the data we need to proceed. We've made more than a dozen requests for the data. In the past three months, I've brought this up

Solving "undiscussables" requires deeper changes to cultural practices, social norms and personal skills.

with you during each of our reviews. At that time you said you would make contact with the Asia V.P...." The facts help the non-engaged sponsor see more clearly what your concern is in a way that's not controversial or accusatory.

Focus on mutual goals. Finally, skillful project managers acknowledge and support common goals. Senior leaders are much less defensive when they know you care about the same goals. This creates an atmosphere of safety, and they're far more likely to respond favorably to your concerns.

David Maxfield is vice president of research at VitalSmarts, Provo, Utah, USA.

Manners Matter

How merely being polite can help your projects run more smoothly.

Yael Cohen, PMP

Once, after attending a meeting with an external stakeholder, I sent a thank-you email on behalf of my team. The stakeholder immediately wrote back, thanking me for my note and saying that if I needed any additional information, she would be happy to supply it. A few weeks later, when I had another request, she remembered me and promptly followed up.

As project managers, we often ask for and receive information, but rarely do we address just how important etiquette is within our profession. In my experience, simple politeness goes a long way toward creating cordial dealings with stakeholders and team members—which also helps projects run better.

Here are four key ways to incorporate courtesy into your projects:

Ask nicely. Using "please," while only an extra word, is likely to score you extra points. I've noticed I am more

inclined to quickly send requested information to courteous people than to those who have been rude to me.

Be thankful. Even if you know you're entitled to the information, you should still be appreciative of the person who provided it. Saying "thank you" will make you stand out from others who don't use common courtesies.

Be respectful. Ignoring requests is not justifiable, even if deadlines are tight and you're juggling competing priorities. If you're not mindful of someone else's time, others are likely to follow suit. I've had team members ask why they have to attend other groups' meetings when people from those groups don't attend my team's meetings. But I still encourage my team members to

In my experience, simple politeness goes a long way toward creating cordial dealings with stakeholders and team members— which also helps projects run better.

attend in the hopes that their respectful behavior will eventually rub off on others.

Offer praise. Acknowledge when you see or hear politeness from your team members. And always try to end a meeting on a praiseworthy note. This can be difficult, but even if the project is going poorly there may be an opportunity to praise your team for continuing to work hard.

Being courteous can create a commonality among stakeholders in disparate disciplines. In project circles, sometimes the functional and technical teams struggle to communicate, but "please" and "thank you" are universal terms that transcend this struggle. They can even help ease tension within the team.

No matter where you are in your career or in a project, it is never too late to employ etiquette and cultivate a respectful and courteous environment.

Yael Cohen, PMP, is a freelance program manager in Denver, Colorado, USA.

The New Sponsor

There's a first time for everything—including project and program governance. Here are five tips for doing it right.

David Tilk, PMP

You've found yourself as the sponsor of a new project—the one that's supposed to change the way your organization does business. Your business unit is going to be one of the most affected areas, so it makes sense for you to take the role. But you've never served as a project sponsor before, and so—apart from applying common sense and calling on past experience—you're not sure what to look out for.

Here are five tips for ensuring your inaugural project or program governance journey is a successful one.

1. UNDERSTAND THE KEY VALUE DRIVERS AND KEEP THE FOCUS ON THE BIG PICTURE

In providing governance over a project or program, one of the most important questions you must answer is, "What is the organization trying to achieve?" That answer is the key to setting the vision for the overall program and to making good decisions. If you're unable to clearly articulate why a project is being undertaken and how it links back to the organization's strategic goals, then the project will likely have trouble achieving benefits.

Own the business case—including the objectives and goals of the project or program—and weigh any future decisions against them. Be sure to take time, even when deadlines are approaching, to see that the business case gets updated with any significant changes before approving them. That discipline will save you from losing focus and eroding value.

2. DEFINE THE STRUCTURES, ROLES, RESPONSIBILITIES AND PROCESSES

One of the most common problems I see with large change initiatives is implementation teams not taking time to set up strong governance. When you're the leader of any governance committee, the first thing to do is ensure the individual members are chosen for their experience and skills. Be sure to assess the steering committee as a whole.

This involves identifying skill gaps and ensuring the body has the right levels of seniority and accountability to be effective change agents. Identifying members who might be out of their depth and working to have adequate representation saves a lot of time in the long run and greatly enhances the chances of project support and success. The next step is to assign clearly defined roles and responsibilities to the committee members.

It's also important that the governance processes and mechanisms are in place, they make sense to you and they fit what you are trying to accomplish. This includes a regular cadence of meetings, understanding how and when the committee will receive information, and determining whether the information will have the right level of detail to help you achieve the business case. Also, documenting roles and responsibilities, structures and processes enables agreement and formal acknowledgement by the major stakeholders.

3. MAKE DECISIONS: DO NOT RECEIVE UPDATES PASSIVELY

Don't allow steering committee meetings to become update sessions. A brief update is fine, but the committee's job is to ensure alignment, give guidance, monitor results, make decisions and clear roadblocks. It's your time to help tackle the tough issues that arise and help the project team stay focused and continue to execute.

It can be difficult to set the direction and pace of a meeting, so make sure you get the right level of information and keep to the right pace of the meeting. Agendas should be focused on decision making and therefore should present the specific questions to be answered by the committee. I've often seen steering committee meetings go overboard with endless discussion and lose sight of the meeting's goal, so it's important to (1) first understand and then follow the agenda of a key governance meeting, (2) set the tone, pace and purpose early in the meeting, and (3) ensure active participation by all members.

4. ASK THE RIGHT QUESTIONS: CHALLENGE, CHALLENGE, CHALLENGE!

You set the vision and agenda for the program and facilitate the steering committee as a governing body. Challenge the project team to think past the upcoming week or month or phase. What are the overall goals and visions of the project? What is the total cost? Is there a bigger end goal or bigger picture? Challenging your

fellow committee members with such questions ensures that a level of robust discussion is reached and a problem is attacked from all angles. Answers to those questions will, hopefully, lead to a more focused project and enable the project team to own its deliverables and execution while you focus on the greater value to be delivered.

You're there for a reason: You and your business unit will be affected by changes. So make sure you're getting value from the project.

5. CONTRIBUTE TO A STRONG TONE AT THE TOP

Steering committee members must be advocates of the project for their teams. Don't underestimate the importance of that advocacy. Make sure your team is well represented for the change and will be prepared by means of an adequate organizational-change work stream. You may have to consider whether the organization's leaders need additional resources or should turn to external advisers to help drive the change within the company. Also factor in the culture of the organization, organizational readiness and ways to most effectively transition to the new way of work.

Ensure your governance peers and leadership are on board and are sending the right messages to their own teams. Your role will be to meet with them personally and enable the organization's leaders to serve as change agents. If you find that receptivity to the change is not working, be prepared to be flexible and to change direction. And always be brave and well informed.

David Tilk, PMP, is a principal in risk assurance, PwC, Cleveland, Ohio, USA.

Lessons Learned

Three things I learned from my executive master of business administration degree.

Suresh Gopalakrishnan, PMP

After a few decades of IT-related project management across a broad set of industries, I recently returned to school for an executive master of business administration degree (EMBA). The 18-month program was rigorous, challenging and exciting. Here are my three big takeaways from the experience:

1. EMPHASIZE TRAITS OVER SKILLS

Traits are innate, but skills can be taught. Often in the recruiting process, too much emphasis is placed on skills and not enough on traits. Organizations—and project managers—would be better served in the long run by focusing more on these traits, known as the five factor model:

1. Conscientiousness (dependable, efficient, achievement-oriented)
2. Emotional stability (calmness, steady, self-confident, secure)

3. Extraversion (sociable, ambitious, active)
4. Agreeableness (courteous, optimistic, friendly)
5. Openness to experience (intellectual, imaginative, analytical)

Individuals with the above traits can overcome certain deficiencies in their skill set, while the reverse isn't always possible. Focusing on the five factor model, more than technical know-how, will help you form a project team that can work well together.

Years back, I interviewed for a project management position at a reputable firm. The interview process was so focused on the specific technical details of the company's system that traits and experience were not explored. I did not get an offer. A year later, I found out that the person who accepted the position—who had a very strong technical background—was let go for not possessing leadership traits.

2. NEGOTIATE BETTER

Throughout a negotiation, it's critical to know three factors: the most desired outcome, the least acceptable agreement (the minimum agreement that stakeholders will accept) and the best alternative to a negotiated agreement, or BATNA (a plan in case an agreement can't be reached). You may start a negotiation with weak BATNA, but the dynamic nature of business events can change that.

A few years back, I was tasked with salvaging a troubled project. Going in, my BATNA position was very weak, and I had no choice but to absorb an unfair share of costs as a demonstration of good faith. A few months into the project, due to some of my corrective actions, project performance improved significantly. However, I failed to recognize the change in my leverage, which

I could have used in my favor and helped save a few thousand dollars.

Another negotiation lesson I learned is to separate interest from position. The classic example is of two chefs fighting over an orange, only to realize that one wants only the juice and the other only the skin. It is impossible to satisfy them both based on their position—they each want the orange. But their interests—why they want it—are different, and a smart negotiator uncovers these and realizes both parties can get what they want. When dealing with conflicting priorities, project practitioners should explore the interests behind stakeholders' positions.

> **When dealing with conflicting priorities, project practitioners should explore the interests behind stakeholders' positions.**

Similarly, remember that negotiations can be win-win, which some call "expanding the pie." One of my professors liked to point out that in many situations we tend to take an "or" approach and lose sight of two additional options. When we say A or B, we forget that there's always the possibility of A and B or neither A nor B.

3. INFLUENCE WITHOUT AUTHORITY

In consulting, one of the biggest challenges is getting clients' acceptance and willingness to share their business processes. Often we encounter people who believe their business is so complex that no one else can understand it. This can lead to many difficulties during the initial stages of a project, such as getting entrance and exit criteria, a complete business scenario listing and detailed requirements.

I once faced a similar challenge on a project: Despite our best efforts, we were not able to get a complete list of business scenarios against which we could test the system we were building. Every time my team requested the listing, we were told, "Our business is so complex that we could only write 15 scenarios. Please keep in mind that there are a million other combinations that we cannot define." Basically we were asked to read the client's mind and build a system that would meet all the requirements. Despite multiple escalations to client leadership, the situation did not improve.

My "Science of Persuasion" course had an interesting equation:

Knowledge + Trust = Authority. Analyzing my challenge in retrospect, it's clear that the project team lacked authority and assumed that escalation would force the client to comply with project needs. Our business analysts did not have a thorough knowledge of the organization's processes, which put us in a very weak position to influence the business. To prevent this situation, project practitioners should spend some serious time understanding business processes so they have an authoritative position from which to navigate a project.

Suresh Gopalakrishnan, PMP, is an engagement manager at IBM, San Diego, California, USA.

Intangible Assets

Stop thinking of emotional intelligence as a mere people skill—it can save projects time and money.

Sam Alkhatib, PMP

I once worked on a team that experienced a major setback after the project manager left mid-project. When the new project manager was named, a team member felt slighted and angry. A longtime veteran with our firm, this employee felt passed over for someone he saw as a relative newcomer.

Blinded by his emotions, he informed our client that the new project manager was unqualified, rendering the team unfit for the work in the eyes of the client. His statements, a mere result of anger, damaged our team's credibility.

This was no way for the team member to prove he was ready to be a project manager, a position that requires poise under pressure. We've all experienced disgruntled team members—or maybe we've let our emotions get the best of us, too. Such situations call for better emotional intelligence (EI).

THE CASE FOR EI

EI, the ability to identify and respond to one's own or others' emotions, is a sound component of any project. Though technical expertise and business acumen matter, project managers with strong EI can better mitigate conflict and build trust with their team members.

In the example above, the project manager had the power to fire the team member. However, an emotionally intelligent project manager recognizes that firing an employee and then hiring and retraining a replacement has a definite impact on project cost and time. In addition to being cost-effective, it is always preferable to solve management issues through coaching and development.

An alternative approach—the one actually taken by the new project manager—was to treat the root cause of the problem. The project manager explained to the upset team member that management's choice didn't marginalize or undermine his efforts. It was a decision made to best support the needs of the project.

This discussion helped the team member realize that the move didn't represent a slight or personal insult. It was purely a business decision. And though the team member acted inappropriately, the project manager diffused his anger, earned respect in the process and retained him as a valuable resource on the project, saving time and money.

THE MAKINGS OF A LEADER

To maximize hiring decisions, organizations should look for these EI attributes in potential project managers:

- Self-restraint, the ability to express negative feelings calmly and sensibly
- Empathy, the ability to recognize emotions in other people
- Communications skills, the ability to facilitate and foster stakeholder relationships

Organizations could use a variety of tests to determine employees' EI levels. The 360-degree assessment, for example, gathers EI feedback from a team member's manager and peers. But an effective, low-cost and less time-consuming method is simply for executives to observe a project manager during the course of a project. Just as a project manager's intelligence is made visible by his or her ability to perform the work, a project manager's emotional intelligence is made visible by his or her leadership ability.

Based on my observations, a project manager with excellent EI saves time and money.

Sam Alkhatib, PMP, is an engineering manager at Cupertino Electric, Inc., San Francisco, California, USA.

A Safe Distance

Take a lesson from parenting—detach to tame the stress of running a project.

Genesh G. Chariyil, PMP

When you're faced with a project challenge, it is natural to get up in the middle of the night and find yourself wondering, "Where did I go wrong?" It's a question parents may ask about their own children.

So as a father, I offer this parental guidance to use when you wake in a sweat and blame yourself for a project's problems: Treat your projects like your kids, and detach from them.

For project managers with grown children, the advice may be easier to grasp. As a parent, you spend much time and energy on your children, but they don't always develop as you hoped. The same can be said for projects. Your hard work and sacrifice don't mean a project will be without flaws. But a sense of detachment can help project managers remain levelheaded when major issues arise.

DEFINING DETACHMENT
Detachment is the art of creating freedom from self-interest or bias, both of which can cloud your ability to make the best rational decisions. During challenging

times, detachment allows you to stand back, analyze the issues with a third-person perspective and discover the right solution.

For example, I worked on a project that was high-risk for schedule delays. I thought I would make myself sick with worry over our missed deadlines. But then I detached, just as I did as a parent. When my children were teenagers, they sometimes came home past curfew. But I couldn't fret about problems with punctuality then—I could only plan for them. Similarly, with the project, I had to expect delays, not fear them.

Detachment also removes the pressure that the problem is something a project manager must fix alone, and a stress-free mind can help you discuss the issues more intelligently with the team members or subject-matter experts to arrive at the best solution.

> **When someone gives constructive feedback on your projects, that person does not intend to blame you personally.**

KEEPING COOL

When stakes are high and money is on the line, it can be hard to detach and remain logical. Just remember that mistakes happen to everyone, and when they do to you, take constructive criticism as an opportunity to improve project performance. This switches the focus from the mistake, which can set you back, to the lessons you learned from it, which pushes you forward.

This advice also comes from parenting. When someone blames your children for their actions, he or she is blaming them and not the way you raised them. Likewise, when someone gives constructive feedback on your projects, that person does not intend to blame you personally.

Projects are never smooth rides. But you can arrive at better solutions for your project challenges by treating your project like your children. Support them, but at the same time, learn to keep a healthy distance from them.

Genesh G. Chariyil, PMP, is a senior project engineer of oil sands at ConocoPhillips Canada, Calgary, Alberta, Canada.

Fake It Till You Make It

A two-step approach to boosting your confidence.

Neal Whitten, PMP

As a leader, are you unsure of yourself? Does a lack of confidence hold you back? All of us have felt this way at some point. But if you routinely think this way, you will undermine your effectiveness, potential and, ultimately, your career. Here's a two-step approach that can help you get past this destructive thinking.

DEFINE WHOM YOU WANT TO BE

Imagine the person you would most like to be. How do you see this person handling various situations? What behaviors does this person demonstrate? For now, don't focus on how hard it might be to adopt these behaviors. Instead, define the vision—the behaviors—that you want to define you. Write them down and commit them to memory. Behaviors that many people desire to hone include: public speaking, conflict resolution, learning when it's okay to break rules, professionally challenging authority, controlling emotions, not taking

things personally, not allowing what others think about you to be more important than what you think about yourself, and taking responsibility for your performance and career.

BE A GOOD ACTOR

Now that you have a vision of your ideal self, become a good actor to transform that vision into reality. Act out—with passion and conviction—the behaviors you most want to mimic. This might sound insincere, but it's how you transform behaviors: You first think about a behavior to adopt, then you act on that thought to replace an old undesirable behavior.

As you act out the behaviors you want to embrace, you will become more confident, deliberate and more likely to be respected by your co-workers. Studies show that exuding self-confidence on the job plays a role in advancing career opportunities.

It's okay to take small steps in the beginning and graduate to larger steps while becoming whom you choose to be. For example, if you have difficulty in speaking to groups or to higher-level management, look for opportunities to present to an individual or a small number of people. Over time, you will become more comfortable speaking to larger groups and authority figures.

As another aid to help you become more confident, imagine you're 100 years old and dying. A young person who admires you says, "What can you tell me that will help me be more successful, including becoming a better employee and leader, and have a more prosperous life?"

How would you respond? Write down the attributes and behaviors that you believe are most important to live a successful life. Then read what you wrote until you've memorized it. You have great advice—now follow it to become the person you wish to be.

Neal Whitten, PMP, president of The Neal Whitten Group, is a speaker, trainer, consultant and mentor.

The Message Is Clear

Adjust communications to break cultural barriers on diverse teams.

Mark Milotich, PMP, and Waseem Hussain

We all know the world functions faster than ever. The speed at which messages from a project manager in Belgium can reach team members in Singapore, for example, can be measured in milliseconds.

This makes globally diverse teams feel like the norm—and it's also made miscommunication caused by cultural differences seem ever-present. We hear of these problems daily. For instance, a U.S. project manager with a diverse team may believe that by having all team members participate equally in the decision-making process, they will be more committed to delivering results. However, when the project manager asks junior Indian team members directly for their opinions during brainstorming meetings via video conference, their replies might often be short and show a lack of engagement, such as, "We can do it the way you want."

These types of communication problems can make for a frustrating project atmosphere. Here's what a project manager should do in these situations:

BE ENCOURAGING WITH REQUESTS

Not every culture views authority in the same manner. Typically, Western cultures value the benefits of involving people in decision-making. However, many cultures in Latin America, the Middle East and Asia prefer clear lines of authority and decision-making.

In the aforementioned example, junior team members in India don't necessarily expect to be consulted for their opinions. Regardless of experience, encourage each team member to act as a leader by using phrases such as: "I would like to hear how you would solve this problem if you were in my position."

FRAME PROBLEMS AS CHALLENGES TO BE SOLVED TOGETHER

In many cultures, people are reluctant to communicate news that could make their boss look bad. Team members may not speak openly about project problems or delays—no matter how many times you ask.

Instead of expecting team members to come forward with problems, frame the discussion so that both leader and followers are on the same side of the obstacle working together toward a solution. For example, don't ask why a project deliverable is late. Instead, let team members know, "I would like to work with you to identify any factors that may cause delays."

AVOID VAGUE TERMS

Project managers are often not aware of the large role that culture plays in how technical or procedural requirements are interpreted. For example, traditions in India's 5,000-year-old culture suggest that a soul has 311 trillion years to fulfill its destiny. This surely relieves some of the pressure of having to deliver a project task by next Tuesday.

Non-specific requests such as "I need that report ASAP" leave room for cultural misinterpretation. "As soon as possible" may have a different meaning depending on what country you come from.

To reduce the likelihood of misunderstanding, create a work breakdown structure with your team. It must include a detailed project dictionary to get everyone on the same page.

Simply because virtual communication such as emails can be sent across the world in a matter of seconds doesn't mean effective messages take no time at all. To deliver results with offshore team members,

"As soon as possible" may have a different meaning depending on what country you come from.

project managers must do more than just think about being culturally savvy. They must actively work at understanding how their own background influences their methods and behavior. With an open mindset, project managers can adapt to the needs of team members with different cultural preferences and practices.

Mark Milotich, PMP, is a founding partner of leadership, communication and change management consultancy Claxus GmbH in Zurich, Switzerland.

Waseem Hussain is the managing director of business strategy consultancy MARWAS AG in Zurich, Switzerland.

Steady the Course

Rely on what you know—even when you're out of your comfort zone.

Midge Crossan, PMP

When Dale Kietzman University (DKU) School of International Development tapped me to teach a master's course on project management for development projects in Douala, Cameroon, I knew it would be an adventure. None of my teaching experience had been with that culture's educational environment. So I turned to my knowledge of project management.

GETTING TO KNOW STAKEHOLDERS

First, my business partner, Debbie Ong, PMP, and I crafted and emailed a questionnaire to our 15 master's students. I needed a good audience analysis, and the way to do so was to get to know each student individually—background, degree, previous project work, etc.

Through this exercise, I learned each had a personal vision for alleviating the suffering of his or her community. These forward-looking, energetic leaders were planning projects that could change the lives of thousands.

Some projects concerned water, sanitation and medicine. Others delved into social causes, targeting at-risk youth or HIV/AIDS orphans and widows. Most project ideas were positioned to trigger a local economic transformation and intended to be sustainable.

BUILDING A CURRICULUM

Cameroon practices an educational method of lecture and memorization. In contrast, we had planned collaborative work groups of four to five students each. The coursework was designed as a sequence of small-group exercises modeled after real project management team meetings and deliverables. I focused the entire curriculum on the basic skills and proven principles of project management.

By sticking to this teaching style, I risked disrupting the students' traditional learning experience. But I thought the course's design could leverage the predilection of adults to learn through personal experience and practical application.

RUNNING THE CLASSROOM LIKE A PROJECT

Soon after landing in Douala, I learned that enrollment in my course had grown from the original 15 students to more than 80, a hodgepodge of graduate students and professionals from 25 to 60 years old. However, I stuck to the original curriculum, which was structured as a chronological voyage through a sample project, anchored by basic project management tools and principles. Students role-played project owners, beneficiaries, project managers and team members. For each lesson, I set up a scenario, explained the exercise, sent the students into work groups to perform a typical project task—such as creating a risk register—and reconvened to critique deliverables. Appreciation for our interactive concept was palpable.

> These forward-looking, energetic leaders were planning projects that could change the lives of thousands.

At the end of every session, students wrote the answers to these questions: What went well today? What could have gone better? It was a lessons learned exercise, both for them on the practice project and for me in the classroom, to know if my teaching was effective.

THE FINAL LESSON LEARNED

I think the main lesson learned for my students was the revelation that transparency, accountability, integrity, mutual respect and work could all be embedded—even proven—through project management.

And for me, I learned that project management has the potential to be a powerful tool for good anywhere in the world.

Midge Crossan, PMP, is the vice president of operations for the Dale Kietzman Academy in Douala, Cameroon and Pasadena, California, USA.

A Wide World

How to work with a diverse, global team.

Anupam Tewari, PMP

For project managers used to working with domestic teams, that first project with team members around the globe can be a shock. Suddenly, you need to gather a fragmented collection of people—who speak different languages, have diverse backgrounds and reside in non-overlapping time zones—into one high-functioning team. Here are some best practices to help ensure the success of your project.

Use Video Conferencing. Of course, much of human communication is nonverbal—through facial expression, gestures and body language. If you're counting on managing your global team only by email and phone, your project is destined for failure. Instead, arrange to have your first all-hands meeting face-to-face. For subsequent meetings, choose the next-best option—video conferencing, which will increase team members' engagement and reduce the chances of miscommunication.

Record these meetings and distribute the recordings with meeting notes. Also, encourage project team members to communicate with both phone calls and emails. Calls bring personality into the communication, whereas emails bring clarity. Use instant messages for quick access to information from team members. Numerous vendors offer collaboration suites, which include meeting, chat and video conferencing tools.

Combine Calendars. The Middle East observes Friday and Saturday as the weekend, and much of the European workforce goes on sabbatical sometime during summer. To keep track of regional holiday and vacation schedules, use tools that let you merge different calendars. Many online meeting applications allow a single global view of calendars from different time zones.

Understand Cultural Differences. In many Asian cultures, saying "yes" or nodding is a respectful way of showing that the listener is paying attention, not necessarily that he or she agrees. Ensure that your team has been trained in cross-cultural communication to avoid misunderstandings that can derail a project. Cultural training videos can be found online. For more formal training, reach out to vendors that offer customized services.

Consider an Interpreter. Though English is the global language for business, strong accents can still impede comprehension. In a business-critical customer negotiation, such confusion can threaten your project. In these situations, it is important to have a language interpreter who can bridge the communication gap. If that's not possible, contact your organization's sales teams—they are usually local and have expertise in the area's languages.

> Though English is the global language for business, strong accents can still impede comprehension. In a business-critical customer negotiation, such confusion can threaten your project.

Include All Team Members. Many remote teams complain that they don't feel included and are given second-rate work. Avoid this by setting clear ground rules at the beginning of the project that outline who will do what work and make which decisions. Also remember to request feedback from your remote team members to ensure that everyone can contribute their expertise. This will also help you match the best-suited individual to a required skill set.

Work Around Time Zones. In one of my recent projects, we had team members joining calls and video-conferences from the U.S., the U.K., Hong Kong, India and Australia. This presented us with the challenge of finding an acceptable meeting time for everyone. We ended up adjusting the meeting agenda so that team members calling at inconvenient times only had to participate in part of the meeting. That helped keep those team members fully involved. Try to rotate which team members have to log in at inconvenient hours. Additionally, explore the possibility of subdividing the teams based on two major time zones.

Be Aware of Local Labor Laws. Remember that local laws or customs could result in additional resource costs. For instance, in many countries, team members who work after 5 p.m. are eligible for overtime. Do your best to facilitate team coordination within reasonable time frames and try to allocate work streams that can be executed around the clock to avoid the extra costs associated with overtime hours.

Anupam Tewari, PMP, is a program manager at Cisco Systems, Washington, D.C., USA.

Building a Dream Team

15 qualities every project manager should cultivate in team members.

Neal Whitten, PMP

If you were building a team and could handpick its members, what are the key attributes you would look for? You say that your team has already been assembled and you have to deal with the cards you've been dealt? That's likely the case for most project managers. But that doesn't absolve you of your duty to lay out a vision to members that makes clear what you expect so that the team can perform its best.

Here are 15 qualities and habits that every leader wants to see in a team member. Of course, members can't be expected to already know or practice everything on the list. Often, these qualities and habits emerge as the team is forming and are reinforced throughout the project. Praise should be heaped on members who demonstrate these traits notably. Members not performing ideally will need coaching so they can move closer to the dream team level.

1. **Participates fully.** Voluntarily speaks up in meetings. Contributes ideas, even if they're unconventional— many times thinking out of the box brings the team to the best solution.

2. **Seeks help.** All of us find ourselves overwhelmed occasionally if we are truly stretching ourselves. Asking for help is a sign of strength, not weakness. Doing so can be a big benefit to a team.

3. **Tells the truth.** It's important to be honest about any obstacles to project progress. When a team member makes a mistake, he or she should admit it and take responsibility. The truth is essential if the team is to function at its peak.

4. **Is reliable.** A team is only as strong as its weakest link, so meeting commitments and consistently delivering quality work is essential. An ideal team member takes personal pride in fulfilling commitments.

5. **Maintains a positive attitude.** Adopts a can-do spirit and looks forward to challenges and opportunities. Doesn't make things personal.

6. **Focuses on solutions.** The most professionally mature members do not engage in finger-pointing. Instead, they focus on solving problems to move forward and recognize that we all make mistakes and need to learn from them, not repeat them.

7. **Is proactive.** Dream team members don't focus just on the task at hand. They look at upcoming tasks to help ensure the team's readiness.

8. **Shares knowledge.** Yes, knowledge is power. But the best performers give it away—they don't hoard it. They recognize how this strengthens the team and raises their own value and reputation in the process.

> **Members not performing ideally will need coaching so they can move closer to the dream team level.**

9. **Takes initiative.** Practices self-reliance when appropriate and requires minimal leadership to make things happen. Understands an assignment and domain of responsibility.

10. **Gives praise to others.** Recognizes the contributions of others and gives credit where due.

11. **Demonstrates integrity.** Integrity is knowing the difference between right and wrong and doing the right thing. It means never giving in to illegal or unethical behavior. Integrity is not optional.

12. **Supports others' ideas.** Team members should be open to the ideas of others. When a decision is made, they should be willing to cooperate with others and support them, even if they originally disagreed with the idea.

13. **Follows the Golden Rule.** Treats others in the same manner as he or she would like to be treated. Practices empathy.

14. **Continuously improves.** Seeks ways to continually improve skills as well as the processes and procedures practiced by the team. Becomes and remains the subject matter expert in a chosen domain and is open to constructive criticism. Doesn't just correct a problem; seeks to correct the process that allowed the problem to occur.

15. **Plays for the team.** Team members have to care about the welfare of the team and its success. They should look out for the team as if its success is defined by each member's actions every day.

This list isn't exhaustive, but it can be a great starting point for team discussion as each point is described and examples are shared to reinforce the benefits to each member and the overall team. I cannot overstate the

I cannot overstate the importance of a team embracing shared values that serve to bond and strengthen the members along their journey.

importance of a team embracing shared values that serve to bond and strengthen the members along their journey.

Almost all project members want to perform well and support the success of the team. They want to mimic behavior that will help the team and, in the process, make them look good as well. As project manager, don't forget your duty to set a consistent example for the team members.

Neal Whitten, PMP, president of The Neal Whitten Group, is a speaker, trainer, consultant and mentor.

Breaking Into Video Games

Competition is stiff when your projects are video games—so plan your entrance into the industry carefully.

Matthew Birken, CSM, PMI-ACP

As a project manager at a video game company, I'm often asked how to break into the industry or how one becomes a project manager in this field.

There's a good reason for these questions. The game industry offers the chance to work in an area that many people are passionate about. And project management is booming, with 15.7 million new project management jobs projected to be created around the world between 2010 and 2020, according to PMI.

Students interested in combining these interests should first research game design schools and programs. When choosing a school, make sure its program is suited to your goals. Do you want to become a technical project manager or an art manager? Do you want to handle client expectations or lead teams? Focus is very important, and being able to demonstrate expertise in a specific area vastly improves your chance of finding a job. In addition to the information you learn in school,

massive amounts of free and premium training are available on the Internet.

Because people skills are so crucial in project management, students should also work on leadership,
emotional intelligence and the ability to trust a team.
Effective project managers need to be skilled in bringing out the best in people, teamwork and intuitive
problem-solving.

Obtaining a professional certification in project management will likely improve your chances of finding a
job. Agile approaches like Scrum are especially popular
in software development. If you're considering becoming certified, I recommend the PMI Agile Certified Practitioner (PMI-ACP)® certification. The certification exam
covers multiple agile approaches, including Scrum, and

their fundamentals. The knowledge you'll gain from preparing for the test is invaluable.

While you're applying for jobs, you can volunteer with game hobbyists or create your own titles. Some great tools for nontechnical people and beginners are Game Maker and Game Salad. These programs feature a drag and drop interface and do the bulk of the engineering work for you. Your first game should be simple and straightforward. It doesn't have to be digital. Design a simple game on paper, then iterate the rules and play again.

Another option is to talk with your local PMI chapter—many of the chapters accept mentees.

Internships are a terrific way to get your foot in the door. Most of the large game studios in the U.S. offer paid internships, but they are extremely competitive. If you're fortunate enough to be offered one, grab it. It's the way I got my start.

An internship will expose you to the building blocks of the game industry, including managing product milestones and deadlines, interacting with team members, creating documents and possibly even leading a small project. It should also be great preparation for your first full-time job in gaming project management.

Matthew Birken, CSM, PMI-ACP, is a project manager at High 5 Games, New York, New York, USA.

Agile Must-Haves

Three requirements for a great agile team.

Gerald O'Connor, MA, MSC, PMI-ACP, PMP

Although agile approaches do not prioritize processes, tools and documentation, agile isn't anarchy. In fact, three factors are required for a great experience with agile.

A GREAT COACH

The agile project manager's role is to facilitate and direct a team to achieve a common vision. To do this well, the project manager must ensure team members have everything they need to best fulfill their role and complete the project's tasks. The project manager should remove anything that may get in the team's way of realizing the project's vision.

A great agile project manager can get the best out of every team member and point the team in the right direction—as well as redirect people when they get off track.

While agile projects do need strong leadership to succeed, the project manager is not necessarily the leader of the team. In fact, the best term to describe an agile project manager is a coach. For example, in soccer, the coach selects his team, analyzes the opposition, prepares tactics for his team and trains them before a game. He guarantees they have everything they need to be at peak performance and that nothing interferes with them. However, the coach does not try to guess every move of the opposing team or plan the team's response. Such a plan would be out of date as soon as it was conceived.

LEADERSHIP

Once the soccer team steps onto the pitch, the coach can only do so much. As the game unfolds, team members take leadership roles at different times.

Similarly, leaders may emerge at different stages of a project. In an iteration focused heavily on design, a team member with strong design capabilities may step up and help the team make the best decisions. For a user story that has a strong database component, a different team member with strength in this area may take the lead.

I once worked as a technical project manager on a project to improve the workflow of producing images for a digital collections website. One user story in the project involved automating the process of aggregating terabytes of images to other websites. We had a tool that could do part of the processing. The problem was the tool would require an end user to spend a huge amount of time creating images. We were trying to modify the tool when a team member pointed out that although completely re-engineering the tool would take more time than modifying it, the amount of time it would save the end user in the long run was exponential. We decided to re-engineer the tool.

This example illustrates both the role of the agile project manager and the team members. The team member had to step forward to a leadership role and use her expertise to guide the team toward the best solution. The project manager had to step back from the details of a problem, hear a completely different approach and judge it on its merits. It is the role of the agile project manager to create an environment that encourages this type of creative thinking—and get out of the way when it happens.

TRUST

A collection of great individuals doesn't automatically make a great team. Great agile teams are built on trust, empowerment and ability. Trust is the most important factor. Team members must trust each other, the project manager and the organization. After trust is built, empowerment is allowing the team to complete its commitments. The least important factor in great agile teams is ability, because a good environment can be an incubator of ability.

When a team is in the formation stages, the strengths and weaknesses of team members will be exposed, creating vulnerabilities. As members learn each other's talents and gaps, they begin to understand and trust each other. That allows each individual's strengths to shine through, and team members will learn to compensate for weaknesses in a teammate.

Teams I have worked on that trust each other didn't have to experience the frustration or negativity that comes from one's ideas not being listened to and encouraged. If a team member points out a way to do things better and the team agrees it is worth pursuing, that team member will be empowered to run with it. Trusting and empowering people to implement changes that will help the group should be encouraged. Having this approach also means members of the team will only suggest ideas if they are willing to follow them through, thus ensuring the suggestions made are practical and well thought-out.

The least important factor in great agile teams is ability, because a good environment can be an incubator of ability.

All of this trust is necessary because when agile teams commit to certain iteration goals, the team as a whole will be judged as having met its targets or missed them—in the same way that the entire soccer team is judged on its wins and losses.

Gerald O'Connor, MA, MSC, PMI-ACP, PMP, has worked as a project manager in the educational and media sectors and can be reached at www.geroconnor.com.

Three Questions

Charged with interviewing project professionals, I learned what can keep a project manager from landing a job.

Miguel Veloz, PMP

A few months ago, the company I work for won a contract for many projects, and we needed to quickly hire several project managers with diverse backgrounds and experience levels. I was assigned to interview 26 candidates in six weeks.

Everyone knew what a milestone is and had a decent explanation of how to plan a project, but I wanted more from candidates.

I wanted project managers who could think on their feet, who were resourceful and able to resolve challenges.

I wanted project managers who cared not only about the results, but also about the journey.

I wanted project managers who paid attention to both the details and the well-being of their teams.

These characteristics should come standard in all great project managers.

As I developed questions, I found that my three favorite questions taught me much about what a great

project professional should avoid saying in interviews. Even the best can be sunk by poor answers.

CAN YOU PLEASE DEFINE "PROJECT MANAGEMENT" IN TWO WORDS?

The question served two purposes: It gave me a quick indication of the candidate's reaction to an unusual request, and it revealed what he or she thinks are the most important characteristics of project management.

Some applicants thought for over a minute before answering, others simply met the question with a puzzled expression and a few impressively responded without hesitation.

A sample of the answers: "Communicate, communicate" showed a willingness to work with sponsors and stakeholders alike. "Manage chaos" proved that the project manager loved a challenge. To me, the follow-up question was the most interesting part: "Why did you choose those words?"

One candidate who said "herding cats," for instance, indicated that he was the type of project manager who likes so much control that it seemed to me the people under him might feel asphyxiated. That's not a project manager who would fit in our organization.

WHAT ARE YOUR WEAKNESSES?

I thought anyone who had prepped for the interview would have an answer at the ready, and his or her preparation would shine through.

Some candidates responded with a weakness only to twist it into a positive. Other answers revealed much about a person's character.

To my surprise, at least a few people said they had "no weaknesses," which I believe indicates either a lack of self-awareness or an elevated ego. One candidate's weakness was "picking up work after people." She explained that if a developer fell behind schedule, she would pick up his or her workload to complete the project on time.

I prefer a leader who learns why the developer is delayed and helps that person improve his or her productivity without shouldering a team member's job.

> I prefer a leader who learns why the developer is delayed and helps that person improve his or her productivity without shouldering a team member's job.

WHAT WOULD YOU LIKE YOUR JOB TO *NOT* INCLUDE?

This question helps identify a candidate's true eagerness for the role and, hopefully, ensures that whomever we hired wouldn't leave in the first weeks after discovering the job wasn't a fit.

One answer stands out: "I can't think of anything I don't like, but I definitely prefer technical work, like designing software." That's not the answer I wanted for the *leader* of a team.

Other responses confirmed the candidates had given the job description only a cursory glance, such as the project managers who applied for a software development position, only to respond that they were better at non-technical projects.

These interviews gave me a different perspective on my own work as a project manager. I was reminded how important it is for us to listen to our peers—even during interviews—and learn from each other.

Miguel Veloz, PMP, is a director and project manager at Fujitsu Consulting in Vancouver, British Columbia, Canada.

Game On

Sometimes seen as just a virtual fantasy world, video games bring project management lessons to life.

Robert Castel, MBA, PMP

To view video games as possessing only entertainment value is short-sighted and without merit.

Today's massively multiplayer online role-playing games (MMORPGs) impart social and innovative learning techniques for individuals and groups on a global scale—and to project management's benefit.

Games, particularly MMORPGs, teach players a plethora of emotional intelligence (EI) competencies, such as self-confidence, empathy, trustworthiness and communication.

Games are not about avoiding reality—they are about experiencing reality in a way that is naturally exploitative at many levels. A project team could very well engage themselves in a game, thereby increasing the EI of the entire team and its chances of project success. If EI is important to project management, then games represent an exciting and practical way for project teams to realize their collective social skills.

For example, in "World of Warcraft" (WoW), the world's largest MMORPG, players around the world assume the roles of heroic fantasy characters completing quests.

WoW's collaborative wiki—an environment of ideas, exploration, and knowledge accumulation and sharing—is second only to Wikipedia in size and is completely user- or player-generated. WoW's wiki, like all

> Games teach players a plethora of
> emotional intelligence (EI) competencies,
> such as self-confidence, empathy,
> trustworthiness and communication.

wikis, is an online learning post where iterative discussions evolve and knowledge management elements materialize for the project team and organization.

For an avid gamer, WoW's wiki can be a research tool and place to reach out to others for extended collaborative engagement. For a project professional, the benefits are equally analogous. More important, a wiki can provide the source to a project's narrative during its life cycle.

Further parallels between WoW, project management teams and EI can be found by focusing on a project's need for collaborative engagement.

In project management, the more a project team collaborates, the greater the likelihood of project success. Similarly, success in WoW requires a collective action and can involve groups of 10, 20 or more players, be they acquaintances or strangers. These "raid parties" form and function similarly to many project teams. In some cases, project managers work with colleagues, and other times, they engage with new people or external organizations. In both gaming teams and project teams, being truly collaborative is the only way to find the project team's intrinsic rewards.

Finally, communication is among one of the most important EI competencies. Within WoW, success prior to and during a coordinated battle with other players requires excellent communication—not unlike the planning and execution sessions of a project. Not all onslaughts with monsters or quests are successful, but players find the combination of communication and adaptive tactical approaches to be absorbing learning experiences. In this regard, project management has a similar experience in the implementation processes.

Robert Castel, MBA, PMP, is the founder of Information Resource Technologies, an IT consulting firm in Toronto, Ontario, Canada.

Meeting With a Mission

How to hold well-run meetings that actually boost morale.

Antoine Gerschel and Lawrence Polsky

In our work with teams around the world, we've found nearly every team has complaints about meetings. But when you're managing projects, meetings are unavoidable.

We recently conducted a survey of 351 businesspeople that found well-run meetings positively correlated to productive teams and happy employees. So what's the key to happier, more productive meetings? Often it is a simple matter of separating your meetings into three distinct types and keeping the content focused on that one type only. Mixing different types invariably creates confusion and frustration, makes meetings lose focus and go overtime, and most important, prevents you from getting the best from your team members.

For instance, a personal check-in, a discussion about a task at hand, a standard status meeting and a brainstorming meeting about improving a process are each

very different. They need different preparation, are associated with very different emotions, and require a different amount of time and discipline.

We recommend you separate your meetings into the following three types:

- **HHAY Meetings**—These are short "hello, how are you?" meetings (seven minutes or less) to check in with fellow project team members and see how each person is doing.
- **Queue Meetings**—These are the meetings to discuss specific issues you have at hand, focused on key decisions that need to be made.
- **Innovation Meetings**—This is time set aside to discuss ways to improve strategy, teamwork, communication or other areas, and/or develop new ideas or processes.

Project meetings can easily be bogged down by HHAY topics and long discussions about how the organization ought to function. Having a separation among these three types will keep your meetings on task, without unnecessary interruptions, without going over time and without participants losing engagement (and happiness).

The more you create meeting happiness, the less your project team will dread meetings. Here are a few more keys to making sure your meetings are on track:

Nine Words: Meeting happiness results when each get-together is effective, efficient and uplifting. When a topic for a different meeting comes up, simply say, "That is a good topic for our ____ meeting." Anyone in the meeting can do it.

Keep Score: Successful people like to experience progress and know what's left to do in order to succeed. You can leverage this to bring out the best in your project team and make meetings a positive time. The simplest and most powerful way to keep score is with your ongoing action item list. As you get things done, don't simply check them off—take time to celebrate successes. Short moments of congratulation and positive reflection feel good, are fun and make the hard work feel worthwhile. Plus, celebration boosts team spirit.

Check in Before You Check Out: High-performing teams take a few minutes to learn and improve. Use the last three to five minutes for a quick "how did the meeting go?" Here's a checklist to help your team evaluate meetings:

Meeting Productivity:

- Were objectives met?
- Did we use our time well?

- Did everyone prepare appropriately?
- Were decisions made, with a good process?
- Do we have clear commitments and action items?

Meeting Happiness:

- Could and did everybody participate?
- Were people concise?
- Were achievement and progress acknowledged?
- Did we follow our rules of staying off devices (laptop, phone, etc.)?

One note: None of these questions are for the HHAY meetings. HHAY meetings are unscripted, no agenda, no minutes, no debriefs. Short and sweet!

Antoine Gerschel and Lawrence Polsky are co-founders of Teams of Distinction, in Princeton, New Jersey, USA.

Make Time for Ethics

Don't let today's rapid-fire project management environment kill your ethics instinct.

Gwen K. Romack, CCEP, SSGB, PMP

Project managers, like other professionals, have seen their everyday working lives shift into overdrive in recent years. Most are expected to carry a smartphone, be accessible nearly 24/7 and make decisions instantaneously. Gone are the days of being able to ruminate on complex challenges and slowly analyze the facts until you reach a decision. Taking time to consider if one of the hundreds of micro-decisions you make every day drifts too close to an ethical line has become a luxury most project managers do not feel they have anymore. And the less time we spend thinking about ethics, the more our instinct to behave ethically weakens.

Many of us like to think we'd make the right call on an ethical issue *if it really counted*. But the day-to-day micro-decisions do really count. Stakeholders notice these decisions, even if you think they don't. Whether you paint a rosy picture of a troubled project's trajectory or

Why not use the [Ethical Decision-Making Framework] prescriptively for at least one decision a week to start training yourself to ask its questions instinctively?

cover for a colleague, micro-decisions can slowly build a stellar reputation or be the thousand tiny cuts that destroy it.

THE PROBLEM

Take the team member who notices you tweaked the forecast due date to be closer to the actual one, or the client who sees that the acceptance testing protocol you used for the final report is not the one you agreed to before testing began. A seed of doubt is planted, and they begin to view all your promises with a trace of suspicion. The client starts wondering if other deliverables will come in as discussed and feels the need to micromanage. The team member doesn't quite believe you when you promise that working hard on the project will pay off, and gradually turns his or her attention to other priorities. Trust is broken. Small issues that could have been solved if you had good relationships become big problems that threaten to destroy the project.

Had you stopped to realize the ethical implications of altering that due date or switching the testing protocol, you might have made a different decision or taken a moment to explain it to the stakeholders to avoid misperceptions.

Unfortunately, the duration and complexity of most projects today means many ethically questionable decisions won't be detected at the organizational level for years, if ever. On shorter, simpler projects, feedback would have come sooner, and we would have had the chance to constantly refine our ethics instinct.

THE SOLUTION

Institutions like PMI have become increasingly active in helping project managers with ethically charged decisions. The PMI Ethics Member Advisory Group developed the Ethical Decision-Making Framework (EDMF) as a practical resource to help project managers think critically and reach an ethical outcome. It's a structured series of questions divided into five areas that help a project manager to navigate the facts, uncertainties and realities of a dilemma in order to take the right action. While the framework is intended to help project managers slow down and analyze what is more likely a macro-decision, it can be used to train our ethics instinct in micro-decisions as well. Why not use the EDMF prescriptively for at least one decision a week (macro or micro) to start training yourself to ask its questions instinctively?

Alternatively, organizations can provide leaders with scenario discussion guides to lead small-group discussions. The guides should engage the team in a meaningful discussion about specific real-world scenarios project teams may face, how their decisions can have unforeseen effects elsewhere, and how to thoughtfully mitigate those effects. Challenging project managers to consider all angles in these scenarios may help them apply the same critical thinking in their day-to-day situations. Another best practice is to tie these scenario discussion guides to the organization's conflict of interest policy.

However it's done, the goal is to start reversing our collective desensitization to the consequences of micro-decisions and retune our ethics instinct. Just as we train ourselves to respond instinctively and correctly in emergency situations, project managers need to ensure a finely calibrated ethics instinct is in place to support hundreds of daily micro-decisions.

Gwen K. Romack, CCEP, SSGB, PMP, is ethics and compliance director at VMWare, Inc., Frederick, Maryland, USA.

Why Project Ethics Matter

Leadership is built on trust. If that foundation is cracked, a project's future is in doubt.

Michael O'Brochta, PMI-ACP, PMP

Once, when a long-term client displayed an ethical lapse, I told him it violated my standards. Then I withdrew as the manager of one of his largest projects. Instead of terminating my contract, the client changed his behavior and also increased his business with my consulting company.

Project ethics matter, and this year's 10th anniversary of the PMI Code of Ethics and Professional Conduct is a good time to reflect on that. Not only do ethics allow us to act in a way consistent with our beliefs, they're a key to executing projects successfully. This is because ethics lead to trust, which leads to leadership, which in turn leads to project success.

A recent study conducted by Vrije University Amsterdam found that the more a leader acts in a way that followers feel is appropriate and ethical, the more that leader will be trusted.

And when people trust someone, they're more likely to follow him or her. As James Kouzes and Barry Posner write in *The Leadership Challenge*, "It's clear that if people anywhere are to willingly follow someone—whether it be into battle or into the boardroom, the front office or the front lines—they first want to assure themselves that the person is worthy of their trust."

Once team members trust a project manager, they can begin to follow him or her. Establishing this

> **Once team members trust a project manager, they can begin to follow him or her.**

leadership is key to solving a challenge that always bedevils project managers: managing people you don't have authority over.

In my case, the client saw me acting ethically, trusted me, then allowed my behavior to lead him toward more ethical behavior—and a successful project.

BEWARE SHORTCUTS

For another example of this process, look at Volkswagen Group. Last year, the German automaker acknowledged manufacturing and installing software to defeat elements of the emission control systems in 11 million diesel-powered cars. It's a massive scandal, a legal quagmire and a huge lapse in ethics, for which the organization has apologized. Many customers have lost their trust in the company. Stock prices and sales of Volkswagens fell drastically after the news broke.

In spite of such negative consequences, ethical infractions abound in the workplace, and employees confront only half of the unethical behavior they see at work, according to *Crucial Accountability: Tools for Resolving Violated Expectations, Broken Commitments, and Bad Behavior*.

Joseph Grenny, a co-author of the book, says the more often people choose to stay silent, the more likely it is norms will shift, ethics will decline and organizations will suffer severe consequences. "While biting your lip may make your job easier in the short term, it does little to preserve productive working relationships and profitable organizations," Mr. Grenny said in a statement. "That's why it's in every employee's best interest to hold colleagues accountable for unethical behavior."

Michael O'Brochta, PMI-ACP, PMP, is chair of the PMI Ethics Member Advisory Group and president of project management consultancy Zozer Inc., Roanoke, Virginia, USA.

Part 2
Technical
Project
Management

Need help "Getting It Done"? In this section, you will find a lot of nuts-and-bolts hints and how-tos on the specifics of running certain types of projects, programs or portfolios. You will find firsthand accounts of practitioners dealing with the immediate aftereffects of disaster and disaster recovery, managing projects in a creative agency, preparing newly formed Olympic Games teams with the data they need and the scope-creep challenges of making a movie. One practitioner tells how he clarified his project schedule by adding a "pseudo resource" called Delay.

The articles in this section cover many of the Knowledge Areas in *A Guide to the Project Management Body of Knowledge (PMBOK® Guide)*. For example, what's the best way to handle positive risks, otherwise known as opportunities? How do you keep risk management processes simple when faced with complexity? What skills do you need to handle the procurement process for sustainable construction projects? How can you do a better job estimating?

In the realm of portfolio management, one of our contributors outlines a framework for prioritizing projects when budgets are unclear.

Another article details a very basic but critically important concern: fitting job safety into the various phases of a project. Not necessarily connected to lack of safety is a column on zombie risks, or retired risks coming back to life. Peruse the following pages for tips to help you on your projects from a technical standpoint.

Myth Busters

Project managers don't stifle the creative process—they help it thrive.

Sarah Flaherty, PMP

As a project manager in the creative department of a large corporation, I spend my days among very imaginative team members.

Creative agencies may not be thought to use project managers the same way an IT or construction organization would. Yet the essence of my role—to produce a deliverable on time, within budget and in line with organizational strategy—remains the same. The only difference is that my field battles a major myth: The creative process trumps project management processes.

Wrong. Process isn't a creativity killer. In fact, project managers can use it to help creativity flourish.

SUPPORT GROUP

Like in any project, I start the initiation phase by relaying the project's specific goals and objectives to team members, who then help me shape how we will reach that goal.

Now is the time to be creative. If my team of designers, writers, developers and print-production specialists doesn't voice possibilities early, I risk wasting time and money on a project with an unimpressive end product.

For example, we recently completed a project to create ad materials for our company to stand out at a college recruitment fair. Our outline started with the tried-and-true method of career-fair advertising: Put a bold banner above our booth and beautiful brochures in front of it.

Yet I knew the team could add value by brainstorming within scope—but without creative boundaries.

Just like I do on all projects, I scheduled brainstorming sessions early for team members to make creative suggestions—and I encouraged them to not hold back. Once we had enough ideas on the table, we discussed the value and limitations of each.

The consensus was to add quick-response (QR) codes to the brochures. These funky-looking squares can be scanned with smartphones, allowing students to access our company's social media posts and microsites—and interact with us long after the career fair was over.

FIGHTING FOR YOUR IDEA

Given the project's limited resources, creating QR codes and microsites could have blown our budget and deadline.

That's when the creative project manager, armed with technical details provided by the team, should schedule a meeting with the sponsor—and fight for the changes.

To ensure buy-in, I focused on two points: Our additions were better aligned with the project's original goal, and the added benefits outweighed the additional costs.

It's up to the sponsor to grant a larger budget for the changes, of course, but generating excitement for proposed modifications is easier when project managers can show that creative measures expand a company's reach.

GROUNDED IN STRATEGY

Once the project's defined, its execution commences just as it would on any other project: Milestones are met based on timelines, schedules and budgets. Work goes through scheduled reviews for approval by various stakeholders.

When it comes to aesthetics, though, a difference of opinion can eat away at the schedule.

As the deadline nears, the project manager's focus must change from encouraging imaginative possibilities to being the authority on whether revisions are grounded in strategy, not subjectivity.

Sarah Flaherty, PMP, is a digital/online engagement project manager contracting with insurance companies and creative agencies in the New York/Connecticut area of the USA.

No Time to Delay

A post-disaster recovery plan must shine with vision and promise to boost investor confidence in rebuilding projects.

Nick Regos

Every day, it seems as if a new headline appears about a devastating hurricane, tsunami or other powerful natural disaster. The Intergovernmental Panel on Climate Change predicts that in the future, storms will be fewer, but stronger. While project practitioners can't prevent natural disasters from intensifying, they can help a community recover.

AT THE READY

"Recovery" has multiple definitions, but it always fits into these phases: emergency, restoration and reconstruction.

Reconstruction means rebuilding so that the affected region returns to the near equivalent of pre-disaster levels, or launching major construction projects that make the community better than it was.

The major difficulty in reconstruction is investor confidence—or the lack of it. Recovery projects need a mass influx of funds quickly, and such a large sum can't and shouldn't come solely from government resources. Private, philanthropic investors also must see the value in the projects you propose. Here's how you can help them do so.

THE NEED FOR SPEED

To ease the concerns of potential backers, clarify what the projects will and will not deliver. The New Zealand government broadly understood this issue after a series of earthquakes in 2010 and 2011 left 185 dead, buildings damaged or destroyed and power supplies cut off in the city of Christchurch. The Christchurch City Council developed a recovery plan for the city's central business

> The scale of devastation, the ongoing disruptions caused by aftershocks in an area and our lack of community consultation were working against us. But the latter, at least, was well within our control.

district. It focused on two components: developing an integrated and inspirational vision for Christchurch, and providing the framework and strategy for how the city would be rebuilt and developed over a 20-year period.

Included in the 65-person planning team were construction, infrastructure and other subject-matter experts (SMEs). But it was project management expertise that would immediately shape the plan.

Because recovery is a lengthy process, council members initially defined the project schedule as a

Cranes dismantle buildings that suffered earthquake damage in Christchurch, New Zealand.

"marathon." However, as the project manager, I realized we did not have time for a long-distance run. The government wanted a recovery plan in nine months. But for the community stakeholders affected by the earthquake's destruction, the sooner we had a plan, the sooner we could rebuild. Therefore, the need for speed was always foremost on our minds.

Due to the tight time frame, we refocused the plan from big-picture milestones into a series of smaller sprints. This allowed us to adapt to SME-suggested changes and create the first draft within five months, enough time for public consultation.

For example, the budget for the final plan was a number we could figure out only with the help of SMEs.

I consolidated their recommendations to identify duplication and interdependencies. Then, we held monthly cross-expertise workshop reviews to discuss where feedback overlapped. For instance, several roads needed repair, as did parts of the sewer system. What we found is that often, these types of projects could work in tandem. If we were planning to reconstruct a road, we would ask ourselves, "Is there a sewer project beneath it?" The answer often helped us control costs and deliver a budget with substantial savings.

ALL FOR ONE

We also used lessons learned from other recovery projects to pave our plan. The need to incorporate lessons learned became more clear when a delegation from our team visited San Francisco, California, USA to meet with disaster-recovery experts. After they reviewed our working recovery plan, we were told the timescales given to deliver it to investors were impossible to achieve.

The scale of devastation, the ongoing disruptions caused by aftershocks in an area and our lack of community consultation were working against us. But the latter, at least, was well within our control.

Instead of trying to retrofit community feedback, we pushed forward with public-stakeholder initiatives, such as 48-hour design competitions for small-scale construction projects. This provided a forum for design professionals outside of our team to contribute.

AND ONE FOR ALL

With one month to spare, our team delivered a 1,195-page recovery plan. It incorporated 56 individual projects and initiatives, and was the largest public consultation program in New Zealand's history.

The feedback we received from philanthropic investors showed they felt confident about where the plan would take us. And with the implementation of a robust project management framework, they were also confident we knew not only how to recover—but also how to emerge stronger than before.

Nick Regos, based in Christchurch, New Zealand, won the 2012 PMI New Zealand Chapter Project Manager of the Year Award for his work on the Christchurch Draft Central City Recovery Plan. He is a director of earthquake and structural engineering company Miyamoto Nexus and Nexus Projects, a project management consultancy.

Mastering the Green Domain

Procurement plays a big role in sustainable construction projects. But it doesn't have to slow down a project.

Ed LeBard, PMP

The trend shows no sign of stopping: Organizations are incorporating more sustainable design into their construction projects to harness energy savings and lessen their environmental impact. To help with these efforts, a growing number of U.S. federal, state and local government agencies are creating procurement programs to promote the use of environmentally sustainable products and targeted energy and water savings on large projects.

The procurement process for green buildings may seem daunting to a newcomer because it requires different team member qualifications and different requirements management. Yet the performance—and bottom-line benefits—of such buildings are impressive.

GREEN TEAM
Green buildings demand more up-front teamwork and open lines of communication between disciplines.

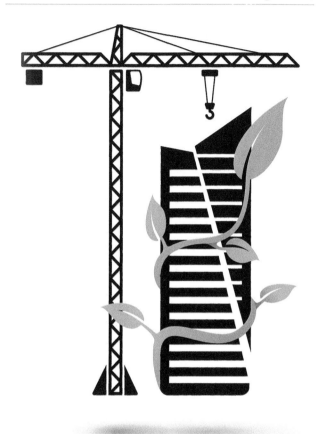

This is because sustainability is a factor not just in the building's design, but in its construction and eventual life-cycle performance too. In addition, many jurisdictions require arduous approval processes to ensure the project conforms with local green building requirements, which may be more stringent than international and state building codes.

The procurement process for green buildings may seem daunting to a newcomer because it requires different team member qualifications and different requirements management.

For instance, on several LEED-certified projects I worked on in Florida, USA, for a retail client, the project team calibrated the design of the walls and roofs to ensure a certain level of insulation around the building and minimize the impact of the region's high humidity. This resulted in efficient HVAC cooling loads during peak and off-peak hours, which translated to sustainable building operations and met local green building requirements. In order to achieve this, early on in the design phase we collaborated very closely with mechanical and electrical engineers as well as the client's construction management team.

This integrated effort for green buildings ultimately pays off via lower life-cycle operating costs (energy and potable water savings), higher productivity with tenants and employees, and higher property values for building owners.

Given the added requirements on the team, it makes sense that more requests for proposals (RFPs) seek teams that already have considerable experience with LEED or Green Globes projects. In addition, more RFP teams want bidders to be experienced with integrated project delivery.

PERFORMANCE PERFECTED

Requirements management during a green building project means detailing exactly what type of sustainability is intended for the project. Procurement may

provide benchmark requirements beyond simply pre-
scribing the level of LEED certification for the overall
project. For instance, project requirements may include:

- Bio-based content
- Enhanced indoor air quality
- Low embodied energy
- Recyclable or reusable components
- Reduced environmental impact over the project's life
  cycle
- Reduced or eliminated toxic substances
- Reduced waste
- Responsible storm-water management to help local
  watersheds
- Sustainable development
- Use of renewable energy or third-party green power
- Water reuse and recycling

Another tack some project sponsors take is to adopt
performance-based goals and leave the procurement
of specific project elements to the project team. The
U.S. General Service Administration and the U.S. Department of Defense, for example, sometimes adopt
performance-based goals that replace detailed specifications and give both the architects and contractors the
opportunity to find innovative solutions that achieve
the performance goals of materials and systems.

Performance-based goals for water systems, for instance, might specify certain water use and savings over
the project's life cycle without mandating specific low-
flow fixtures, vacuum sewage treatments or drip irriga-
tion. On green building projects, performance-based
goals could range from energy and electrical systems

to exterior structural components to interior decorative elements.

These project performance-based design goals are complemented with a project manual indicating performance, descriptive and open (nonrestrictive) specifications. Performance specifications set the aim to be achieved—not the means of achieving it. Descriptive specifications provide a written detail of a product's properties without the use of trade or brand names. Open specifications encourage competition between vendors or manufacturers by specifying that the quality must be equal to certain brand names.

Having all these types of specifications in the project manual could confuse the general contractor. To minimize that risk, the architect and consultants can instead provide a basis of design listing acceptable manufacturers. The general contractor can share the basis of design with the subcontractors to find the most cost-effective green products that contribute to the sustainable principles of the project. This gives the design and construction teams the flexibility to find innovative solutions that support the performance goals of the project.

Ed LeBard, PMP, is a project manager and architect in the Washington, D.C., USA office of Gensler, a global design firm.

Olympic-Sized Effort

Lessons learned from working on the 2016 games.

Adriano Mota, PMP

When I joined the organizing committee for the 2016 Olympics in Rio de Janeiro, Brazil, I quickly learned that my 10 years' experience managing technology-related projects would only help me so far.

All projects are unique, but planning the summer Olympics might be in a category by itself. Over two weeks in August 2016, 10,500 athletes will compete in 300 events at 33 venues around Rio. Roughly 7.5 million tickets will be sold, and 60,000 volunteers need to be organized. Technology deliverables include mobile, fixed, Internet and cable communications at the competition venues, media centers and athlete accommodations. In addition, the final delivery date is not negotiable, large sums of public and private-sector money must be aligned, and the technology required to successfully deliver the games keeps changing.

Headquarters of the organizing committee for the Rio 2016 Olympic and Paralympic Games

Furthermore, all this has to be done with a team that only recently formed. Working on this massive initiative can feel like being at a startup company.

To help with these challenges, the international Olympic officials provided our team with a vast amount of data from past games, technical manuals detailing deliverables, a very high-level master schedule and a great knowledge-transfer program that allows us to observe all Olympic Games held between our selection and our final delivery.

This knowledge-transfer program covers the whole event scope, including transportation, accommodations, technology, logistics and the obvious items associated with the sports (arenas, medical services, media coverage, fans, etc.). International Olympic officials are careful not to mandate how we should do tasks but rather state the final outcome that is expected from us. This method respects the local organizing committee, the host country's culture, the budget and the execution strategy.

Another tactic we employed to help manage the vast and complex amount of work was to bring in people with Olympic planning experience. However, their experience is not always wholly applicable, and sometimes a hybrid method has to be worked out. For example, during past Olympics, staffing for venues that require someone to be on duty at all times was often arranged by setting up two teams to each work 12-hour shifts. However, this is not currently allowed under Brazilian labor law, and we will have to come up with alternate plans.

As the project moved ahead, we began to realize another challenge: how to allow for the team's dissolution just after the project delivery date while maintaining the team's focus.

Our project team is facing unemployment once the games are delivered—or even sooner. In addition to creating insecurity among team members, this also means that the organization loses the power to attract the best resources to the project as we get closer to the Olympics, since not many people will change their current jobs and risk unemployment a year or six months down the road.

To cope with these problems, we adhere to the organization's solid delivery plan and rely on a cohesive staff engaged with the plan and strong managers who drive the teams to deliver tasks while reassuring people that they will have a smooth transition to a games-time operations role.

On a personal level, each team member needs to have a little reality check: No job comes with any warranty that it will last forever. Furthermore, team members can remind themselves that working on the Olympics is a once-in-a-lifetime opportunity that may be worth whatever job-related uncertainty follows it. For me, the Olympics has brought the experience of discovering a whole new project environment, being fully engaged in it and creating a new personal baseline for my next project.

Adriano Mota, PMP, is the service directory manager for the Rio 2016 Organizing Committee for the Olympic and Paralympic Games in Rio de Janeiro, Brazil.

You Get the Picture

Project managers learn the challenges of making a movie.

Rhonda Wilson Oshetoye, PMP, and Laurence Cook, PMP

Making a movie is a project. Yet when our project management firm undertook a film for the first time, we could find little information about project management in the movie industry. Instead, we had to discover on our own how to implement project management methodologies in this field.

When BJG Media Productions hired us for the indie film *A Choice to Yield*, our project managers facilitated the initiation discussion with stakeholders. Once stakeholders agreed on the scope and budget, the team began the initiation process.

Planning was a nightmare at first, as we tried to learn the ins and outs of moviemaking. With minimal guidance and without historical documents, the team struggled to understand the depth and cost of every task. We learned through intense research that the closest position to a project manager is the line producer. Once the

line producer responsibilities became clear, planning began to roll. Planning sessions shifted to risks.

We created a risk management plan with high-, medium- and low-risk factors and associated costs for each. From changing actors to planning the use of venues, the cost of change is a huge variable for movies. One venue change can cost up to US$15,000 for a three-hour shoot. The tension between the director's vision and the reality of managing the budget for unknowns is a serious issue, and managing the director became the highest and most costly risk of the entire project.

A STRICT BUDGET FOCUS

Project plans had to be solidified before the first scene could be shot. We broke the plan into phases. From there, our team planned everything from the script review to the casting call, identified resources, procured equipment and enacted a communication plan. We planned movement from set to set, coordinated with a caterer and signed venue contracts.

Next, we distributed the shoot schedule and wardrobe requirements to each actor, gaffer, cameraman, associate director and other production support personnel.

Project execution entailed early morning pre-shoot meetings and post-shoot assessments of the shots—including immediate lessons-learned discussions, schedule adjustments and revalidating resource assignments. This process enabled us to manage every aspect of filming with regard to contract agreements, set requirements and payment distribution.

The need to reshoot scenes required significant adjustments to the schedule and budget. While we'd expected some reshoots, we didn't expect as many as were required. This sent the budget spiraling, and pushed us back to planning. To mitigate cost and overages per scene, we made specific adjustments for future shoots. We reduced lighting costs by shooting night scenes during the day and simplified makeup requirements. We also had to renegotiate a few contracts, make backdrop construction changes on location and modify venue-use agreements. As with any project in execution, budget awareness took precedence and required strict focus.

In moviemaking, the unknowns are huge and unpredictable, but the project manager's skills and training are a great fit for managing the process.

This paid off when the project was successfully completed 2 percent under budget. In addition, our firm has been asked to manage another movie project.

Of the many skills project managers bring to the film industry, the most important are managing change and controlling the supporting tasks of filming. The orchestration of multiple moving parts requires a project manager's ability to adapt and overcome obstacles. In moviemaking, the unknowns are huge and unpredictable, but the project manager's skills and training are a great fit for managing the process.

Rhonda Wilson Oshetoye, PMP, and Laurence Cook, PMP, are practicing partners at RLO Enterprises, Atlanta, Georgia, USA.

Mobile Plan

How to prepare for an enterprise
mobile app project.

John Pitchko, PMP

Many people mistakenly believe that deploying mobile services in an organization is easy. The widespread adoption of mobile technology leads users to believe that creating an enterprise mobile service is as simple as downloading an app from the app store. What many business users fail to understand is that the app itself is only one aspect of the entire mobile solution. When planning to deploy mobile projects, project leaders need to keep the following two points in mind.

KNOW YOUR INFRASTRUCTURE CAPABILITIES

When workers at our oil sand mine expressed interest in deploying a mobile app to support their work, we investigated their base infrastructure before looking deeply at the app itself. Our analysis quickly identified a

number of roadblocks: poor Wi-Fi coverage and budget concerns about tablets and ongoing cellular data fees. Had this analysis not been performed, money would have been spent to provide a mobile service usable by only a small number of workers. Our work now focuses on building a longer-term road map of mobile technology and services for that mine and building support from the various stakeholders to implement it.

If your mobile project also involves workers in the field, a reliable Wi-Fi or cellular network connection may not be available. Workers' devices will likely require a weather-proof enclosure and, in some cases, an anti-spark certification. For more traditional mobile projects in an office, users typically have a secured wired or wireless connection that connects their computer to the organization's network. In that environment, mobility can be achieved by deploying standard tablets or smartphones connected to the organization's Wi-Fi. Regardless of location, users may require the use of a VPN to allow secure access to the organization's networks. All these infrastructure factors need to be considered when analyzing the feasibility for mobile projects, and may ultimately dissuade sponsorship of the project.

HAVE A SOLID BUSINESS CASE

Workers at some of our remote well sites had no easy way to access data. One option was to purchase a ruggedized laptop, but these were expensive and could not be easily used at the well sites. We created a solution that involved deploying iPads and several streamlined mobile apps that presented the precise information needed by the workers as they were working on the well head. Because this solution was less expensive and functioned well, the business case was easy to make.

The app itself is only one aspect of the entire mobile solution.

Other organizations may also find that they can save money by replacing more expensive traditional desktop or laptop computers with basic tablets. Another source of value is reducing worker travel time—putting information and technology at a user's job site allows him or her to spend more time at the site and less time behind a desk. Less travel also provides safety benefits as workers spend less time driving a vehicle.

Keeping these items in mind will help ensure a successful launch of an enterprise mobility project. Without a robust business case and an understanding of infrastructure capabilities, a mobility project will struggle to gain momentum. As mobility becomes even more present in the world, enterprises able to rapidly roll out mobile technology will outpace those that cannot.

John Pitchko, PMP, is founder of Pitchko Technology in Calgary, Alberta, Canada, and a former program manager for an energy company.

Simpleminded

When faced with complexity, keep risk management processes simple.

Len Pannett

Poorly executed risk management can result in spectacular project failures. Think deep-water oil spills and nuclear reactor meltdowns.

But well-executed risk management on megaprojects can lead to incredible success stories—and great examples for future projects. The US$23 billion Crossrail project, a 73-mile (118-kilometer) transit line being built through and underneath London, England, is a great case in point.

THE FORCES BEHIND BAD RISK MANAGEMENT

With so much potential for greatness, where does risk management go wrong? Usually, its benefits begin to suffer when risk management techniques are performed just to comply with organizational standards. This is when risk management turns into mere "risk appreciation"—the creation of a long list of risks without

thought-through action plans to address them, or a narrow focus on financial consequences without regard to delivery.

In short, bad risk management happens when it is implemented without meaning and without visible benefits to stakeholders.

On projects with added complexity, strategic oversight in risk management grows increasingly difficult. Megaprojects, by the very nature of their big scale and

In short, bad risk management happens
when it is implemented without
meaning and without visible benefits to
stakeholders.

budgets, often require joint ventures for funding. That's
a lot of stakeholders with numerous—and possibly
conflicting—views at the top. With so many hands in
the pot, such collaboration spurs ever-changing legal
conditions and complicated supply chains.

But while there's much noise at the top, the project focus
remains on delivering an end product that makes customers happier. In Crossrail's case, that's providing a rail service
that improves the travel time for London commuters.

Such challenges can sometimes place risks in the
back of project professionals' minds, and risks will just
vanish into a process black hole. Rather, project professionals must be able to provide visible evidence that
the risks are under control. "Good risk management
supports delivery, provides assurance and enables informed decision-making," Rob Halstead, Crossrail's head
of risk management, told me.

CAN IT ALL BE SO SIMPLE?

No "one-size-fits-all" solution exists to achieve strategically driven risk management, but lessons have already
emerged from the Crossrail project. The overall take-
away: When faced with complexity, keep risk management processes simple.

The market is awash with tools to help collate, analyze and report risks. But Mr. Halstead has found more
success by effectively using established approaches
and tools at the outset, and only introducing innovative
solutions once everyone is comfortable with the basics.

Conventional methods also allow experienced team members who already have a project management knowledge baseline to detect and handle risks in a consistent, immediate manner. In turn, this promotes greater reliability and clarity of risk information from the beginning.

Another simple and effective part of risk management is risk review boards—comprised of independent, senior-level technical, operational, financial and organizational representation who challenge project managers to recognize, understand, prioritize and control risks by supplying an objective, third-party input.

Because it isn't feasible to tackle all risks from every source with equal focus, these boards help project professionals home in on the risks most directly impacting the project's objectives.

These can then be tied to team and individual incentives for added impetus. For instance, Crossrail identifies the top 100 risks every year, using this process as a key performance indicator to help determine bonuses and thereby engaging project managers in the risk management process.

By ensuring that risk management is kept simple and making it a process that project stakeholders strive to excel at, projects will increasingly be celebrated for providing the right deliverable at the right time with the right budget.

Len Pannett is a partner with Visagio, an operational strategy consultancy involved in the engineering and technical industry sectors in Europe, Brazil and the United States.

Crisis Mode

How preparation and innovative thinking can save projects during an emergency.

Joan Landry, PMP

Abbott's crisis management team monitored Typhoon Haiyan in 2013 just as we had any other hurricane or typhoon. We followed its intensity and path. We reached out to our employees in the Philippines to ensure everyone was prepared. The country is hit by many typhoons each year; people seemed ready.

But then the storm, known locally as Yolanda, intensified as it bore down on the Luzon region. Although the area was prepared for a typhoon, no one was prepared for the Category 5 super typhoon and the devastation it brought.

As a project manager, what can you do to prepare for crisis events?

First, use your professional planning and risk management skills to help prepare yourself and your family for a possible crisis. Many government websites provide guidelines; in the United States, www.ready.gov is an

Typhoon Haiyan, which devastated parts of the Philippines in 2013, was one of the biggest typhoons to ever hit land.

excellent resource. Common elements of preparation include:

- An emergency kit (three days of food, water and other emergency supplies)
- A family communication plan (contact information, where to assemble if you cannot reach each other by phone or text)

Second, you need to consider risk and contingencies for your project plan. If a risk to project activity has a high likelihood of occurring and a high impact if it does occur, you may want to look at contingency planning for that activity.

IN THE AFTERMATH

After a devastating natural disaster or other crisis, it might seem unfathomable to focus on work. Yet recovery efforts start with identifying and prioritizing projects. Once you know you and your family are safe, check in with your team members to find out if they are okay. Has anyone in their family been affected?

Now look at the damage. How has your project been impacted? Are these areas that have been previously identified as high-risk? Do you have contingency plans already in place? What are the options? How can your team recover quickly? What does your team need to do temporarily? What permanent change is needed to the project?

Allow your team to come up with creative solutions to solve these problems. After Superstorm Sandy struck the northeastern United States in 2012, Abbott technical support staff needed to visit hospitals in Manhattan, New York, to service equipment. There was just one problem: Most of the gas stations in the area were unable to pump gas because they had no electricity. The technical staff could not drive into the city, and public transportation was unavailable.

We seemed out of options until a member of the team had a clever idea: rental cars. Rental cars come with a full tank of gas, and there were a lot of them available. Once the fuel tank got low, team members could bring the car back and rent a different one. This allowed our technical staff to bridge the gap until power was restored—almost two weeks later.

As for our workers in the Philippines, we were happy to learn that—due to prior planning, quick decision-making and luck—all employees in the impacted region were safely evacuated.

Joan Landry, PMP, is program manager of crisis management and global business continuity at Abbott, Abbott Park, Illinois, USA.

Stressing Safety

From simulations to walk-throughs,
project safety should be front and center.

Raymond Jasniecki, PMP

I once worked on a US$6 million project to remove a piece of highly contaminated equipment from a commercial nuclear plant, load it into a specially designed container and transport it over public roads for disposal. Understandably, safety was top of mind throughout the project.

Yet it's not only nuclear projects that carry a sense of danger. Practitioners in sectors like infrastructure and energy also have a heightened responsibility to make sure work is accomplished safely. To get a handle on this, project managers divide worker safety into three phases: planning, executing and controlling.

During the planning phase, the project manager must ensure that a job safety analysis (JSA) is performed and approved. The JSA analyzes all tasks and activities in the work breakdown structure to look for potential hazards, and then identifies methods to

eliminate or reduce those hazards. The methods should be easy for workers to understand and should strive first to eliminate the hazards, and second to minimize consequences to workers.

The project team should maintain a healthy questioning attitude during the planning phase, asking questions such as:

- What are the critical activities?
- What mistakes might be made?
- What is the worst that could happen?
- What defenses should we use?

Planning should include a review of previous similar jobs done by the team. The project manager also should double-check that an adequate emergency plan

> While safety begins with the individual, the project manager must use his or her planning, communication and leadership skills to instill a mindset that safety is paramount.

is developed and approved. This plan should include emergency contacts, directions to the nearest hospital and information on whether specialized training will be necessary for workers.

Some projects may require even more planning. For the nuclear project I worked on, our project team tested the maneuvers with simulated mock-ups, in addition to the steps detailed above. The result was that the project was completed safely and within the established constraints.

MAKE YOURSELF VISIBLE

During the next phase, execution, the project manager should "manage by walking around"—by being a visible presence at the job site. Whenever the project manager is at the site, he or she should perform a quick review of the work location and the tasks to be performed. Are there visible hazards? Could workers get hurt? Are there different conditions than what were planned for?

Each day, the project manager or an appropriate team member should hold a pre-job briefing. This should include a team walk through the work area to review site-specific conditions. Workers should document their attendance at the pre-job briefing to establish accountability. This briefing will also:

- Emphasize safety over urgency
- Ensure each worker fully understands assigned tasks

- Identify specific hazards and error-prone situations and how to avoid them
- Review lessons learned

Part of the project manager's responsibility for safety includes making sure the team develops and maintains proper safety habits. Personnel should be encouraged to use the STAR technique (stop, think, act, review). Team members should not accept anything at face value but instead should challenge assumptions, confirm details when uncertainty exists and investigate conditions that don't appear to be correct. If a condition arises that is different than the one for which work steps were developed, stop immediately and place the work area in a safe configuration.

While safety begins with the individual, the project manager must use his or her planning, communication and leadership skills to instill a mindset that safety is paramount.

Raymond Jasniecki, PMP, is a project team leader at KBR in Circleville, Ohio, USA.

Risks Aren't Always Negative

Planning for positive risks means you're in position to take advantage of opportunities.

Christian Bisson, PMP

The word "risks" carries a negative connotation, which is why project managers tend to believe risks should be mitigated or avoided as much as possible. But that common belief means you may be missing out on opportunities.

A negative risk is a threat, and when it occurs, it becomes an issue. However, a risk can be positive by providing an opportunity for your project and organization.

This is critical to consider when registering your risks.

Let's say your organization is rolling out a new website; an example of a positive risk would be having too many visitors. A large amount of site traffic would be great, but there is a risk the servers won't be able to handle it.

The risk management processes are the same for positive risks as for negative ones: You still need to identify risks, assess their impact on your project and

monitor them throughout the project. But instead of mitigating, avoiding or transferring positive risks, you'll want to enhance, exploit or share them.

ENHANCING THE RISK

Enhancing a risk is planning and acting so that the risk's probability or impact rises. The idea behind enhancing is identifying the source of a risk and planning accordingly.

In the website roll-out project, you could identify that to have many visitors, you need people to share it via social media. Therefore, your planning includes making sure it's easy to share everything on the website (by adding share plug-ins, for example). In addition, you make sure to use calls to action to have people follow you on Facebook, Twitter or other relevant social media platforms.

By doing so, not only do you raise the probability that more people will go on your organization's website, but you also raise the impact by gathering new followers on social channels, which you can leverage in the future.

EXPLOITING THE RISK

Exploiting a risk means going beyond enhancing it. It's taking proper actions to make sure the risk becomes an opportunity.

Normally, you would plan to mitigate a risk by listing concrete actions to prevent it. But when exploiting a positive risk, you'll plan to make it happen.

There is a lot of confusion between enhancing a risk and exploiting one, especially because both strategies do affect the probability of the risk hap-pening. The key difference is that enhancing is raising the probability, while exploiting is making sure it happens.

For example, you could plan a media blast to attract people to the website or prepare a social media cam-paign to drive more traffic. You could also make sure that the servers can handle the extra traffic by using cloud hosting.

> Exploiting a risk means going beyond enhancing it. It's taking proper actions to make sure the risk becomes an opportunity.

SHARING THE RISK

Sharing a risk means to have a third party also benefit from the opportunity. The rationale behind this strategy is that your organization may not be able to benefit fully from the opportunity because it lacks the resources of a third party.

For example, you and a third party might plan a contest where the third party offers to give a quantity of its product for free as the prize, while you take care of hosting the contest on your website on launch day. Here, the third party would benefit through contest participants' awareness of its product, and you would gain followers, subscribers or visits through a great prize.

ACCEPTING THE RISK

Accepting the risk is applicable to both negative and positive risks. Basically, you take no action to prevent or enhance the risk and accept that it may happen. In our example, this could mean that if too many users visit the website at once, they will be redirected to a page asking them to come back later because of heavy traffic.

It may seem strange to accept a positive risk without trying to do more. But remember: Enhancing or exploiting a risk comes with a cost—you have to take action and use resources that your organization might not have or that are needed for another project. In that case, you might decide to accept a certain risk and maybe focus on another risk.

When identifying risks, do not concentrate only on negative elements; think of all the opportunities that are available and plan to exploit or enhance them. By focusing solely on the negative, you will miss out on many opportunities.

Christian Bisson, PMP, is senior project manager at Mirum, Sainte-Julie, Quebec, Canada. He blogs at Voices on Project Management, ProjectManagement.com.

Zombie Risks

How to prevent retired risks from coming back to life.

Rex M. Holmlin, PE, PMP

I teach project management to undergraduate and graduate students, as well as students in continuing corporate education programs. During one class on project risk management, we discussed retiring risks once the activities associated with them were complete. That's when a student asked, "What about zombie risks?"

He had worked on a project in which the team diligently identified risks and included them in the risk register. As the likelihood of each risk became low enough, the team retired it, and the contingency funds set aside for that risk were freed up for other purposes.

Unfortunately, after being retired, one risk "came back to life"—much like a zombie—and was realized. At this point, the funds associated with the risk response plan had been used for other purposes.

In our discussion about zombie risks, three important points emerged. First, project risk management

tools should be integrated with other tools we use in project management to provide a better understanding of interdependencies. One option is to map risks to either the work breakdown structure (WBS) and/or the project schedule. (For more information on this, see the PMI Global Congress paper *Understanding Risk Exposure Using Multiple Hierarchies* by David Hillson, PhD, PMP, PMI Fellow.)

By mapping risks to the WBS, we know which deliverables have risks associated with them. We also get a much better idea about where clusters of risk may lie in our project. A project team could map risks directly to activities in the schedule, but there is potential value in taking a "top-down" approach and mapping to the WBS first. While risks may be primarily associated with a particular activity, mapping to the WBS and then decomposing deliverables into activities could better identify other relationships or dependencies.

A second theme in our discussion on preventing zombie risks was the need for a structured process for risk retirement and the release of funds associated with the risk. When should a risk be retired? When the activity it is primarily associated with is complete? Or when a deliverable the activity is associated with is complete? Making this decision takes considerable judgment, and organizations could benefit from a formalized discussion about risk retirement, as well as a documented risk retirement process.

Lastly, the discussion stressed the importance of the role of risk owner, the project team member who is charged with monitoring and managing a particular risk. The risk owner should have a very clearly delineated role to play in recommending risk retirement and requesting release of contingency funds associated with that risk.

With these processes in place, project teams can make sure their risks won't come back to haunt them after they've been retired.

Rex M. Holmlin, PE, PMP, is a clinical professor of project management in the Mason School of Business at the College of William and Mary, Williamsburg, Virginia, USA.

Predicting the Unpredictable

How to analyze project risks using event chain methodology.

Lev Virine and Michael Trumper

Federation Tower is one of the largest construction projects in Moscow, Russia, but it has had a troubled history. The project team initially planned a 62-story west tower and a 93-story east tower, with a 506-meter spire in between. In 2008, the west tower was completed, but work on the partially built east tower was suspended due to lack of funding. Construction resumed in 2011, but the halt had caused technical issues that had to be fixed. The next year, a fire delayed the project again. Then a main contractor was replaced. In 2014, stakeholders decided to demolish the partially erected spire, change the design and increase the number of floors to 95. The plan is now to complete the tower this year.

Project managers viewing this troubled project might wonder: Could improved risk management have prevented any of this delay and rework? Fortunately,

By accurately estimating the probability and impact of risk drivers, we can create a risk-adjusted project schedule.

modern risk analysis techniques allow us to create an accurate project forecast with ranges that account for risks and uncertainties. By accurately estimating the probability and impact of risk drivers, we can create a risk-adjusted project schedule. Analyzing this schedule provides us with answers to very important questions: What happens to the schedule if certain risks occur, and what is the chance that the project or a certain milestone will be completed on time and on budget?

In the case of Federation Tower's east tower, the delays and extra costs were caused not only by separate events, but by chains of events: The global financial crisis led to the suspension of construction, which eventually caused design changes and the decision to demolish the spire. Such event chains may lead to a dramatic escalation of project costs and major delays.

So the next step toward a better modeling of project uncertainties is event chain methodology. This focuses on analyzing the relationship between events: Events can trigger other events, which may require mitigation and response activities that create their own events. Event chain methodology also helps us perform a risk analysis of portfolios, since the same risk can affect different projects.

It might sound complex, but it doesn't have to be. Here is a brief outline of how to perform event chain methodology:

Event chain diagram

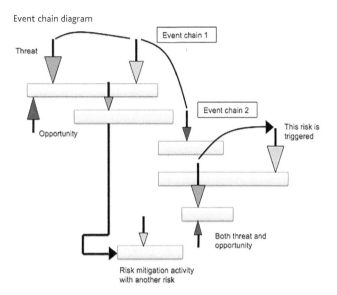

Risk mitigation activity
with another risk

1. Design schedules for projects within a portfolio.
2. Identify risks and enter them into the risk register. Risks may have different properties, including costs.
3. Assign risks to activities and resources. During this stage, the risk probabilities and impacts can be defined. The same risk, assigned to different activities and resources, may have different probabilities and impacts. The same risks also may belong to different categories: For example, the risk of fire may impact safety, cost and schedule.
4. Identify risk mitigation and response plans and associate them with activities on project schedules. These response plans may have risks themselves. For example, during the Alaskan Way Viaduct Replacement project in the U.S. state of Washington,

a tunnel-boring machine broke. To repair it, a 120-foot vertical shaft had to be drilled down to the machine's cutting head. This risk response project delayed construction for more than a year.

5. Identify relationships between risks and determine event chains. Risks can trigger each other or be correlated with each other.

6. Create an event chain diagram (like the one on the previous page), an easy way to visualize event chains. Threats and opportunities assigned to the activities are shown as arrows on the Gantt chart. The size of the arrow depicts risk probability. The color depicts impact.

7. Identify uncertainties in project activities that are not part of the discrete risk events, and define their cost and duration using three-point estimates (best case, most likely and worst case). For example, the quality of concrete has delayed many construction activities. This delay can be modeled using three-point estimates of the duration of affected activities.

8. Perform Monte Carlo simulations of project schedules. This means project schedules will be calculated multiple times with different combinations of events.

After the calculation is performed, the analysis allows us to:

1. Create a risk-adjusted project schedule. The schedule can be associated with a certain probability that a project will be completed on time and on budget. We can also determine a probability that certain milestones in terms of cost and schedule will be met.

2. Rank risks based on their cumulative probability and impact on multiple activities and resources. Higher-ranked risks can be mitigated or avoided first. Event chain methodology allows the ranking of risks belonging to different categories separately or the calculation of a combined ranking based on the relative importance of different categories. We can also identify critical event chains, which can be broken if necessary.

3. Rank projects in a portfolio based on their risk exposure.

4. Identify the probability that certain mitigation and response plans will need to be executed, so these plans can be determined in advance.

Modern software significantly simplifies risk analysis of portfolios. Risks can be constantly tracked during the course of projects. A risk's probability and impact may change over the course of a project; therefore, project and portfolio risk analysis should be performed on a regular basis. The main advantage of project risk analysis is that, if done properly, it provides realistic project schedules, and improves both the quality of project decisions and project outcomes.

Lev Virine is a consultant at Intaver Institute, Calgary, Alberta, Canada.

Michael Trumper is business development manager at Intaver Institute.

7 Tips for Estimating Your Projects

Take the subjectivity and speculation out of estimating.

Christian Bisson, PMP

Estimating can be a tedious task, and the final numbers are influenced by a daunting number of factors: scope, type of project, resources involved in estimating, type of client, unknown variables, potential risks and more. But estimating is critical to your project's—and your organization's—success. These tips can help practitioners arrive at an estimate that's both useful and accurate.

1. ALWAYS INCLUDE CONTINGENCY

A contingency is something that's expected to be spent. Therefore, project managers shouldn't remove it from an estimate simply to make the project look less expensive. In addition to a monetary contingency, also include the time and resources needed to handle the work the contingency implies.

If the contingency is not needed, the project will simply be done earlier and the organization can keep the funds for another time.

2. AVOID MAKING NUMBERS FIT THE BUDGET

When working on an estimate, a project manager might be tempted to pressure the team to keep the numbers optimistically low. But this creates an estimate that is only good on paper; when the time comes to justify an overage, the team members will simply reveal that they were asked to estimate low numbers and overage should be expected. If the budget and scope are at odds, practitioners should instead adjust the scope: Ask the team to provide what can be done within the budget.

3. COMMUNICATE TEAM ASSUMPTIONS

A common mistake when estimating is listing tasks and numbers while not specifying assumptions behind the numbers. For example, team members may say they can create an online form in seven hours, but they're envisioning a form with 10-12 fields, while you are expecting 20 fields. Employ good requirements management by making sure team members provide clear details on what they're estimating to avoid costly surprises later in the project.

4. AVOID USING ONLY HIGH-LEVEL BREAKDOWNS

The more detailed the breakdown, the more accurate the estimate and the easier it is to get the whole team on the same page. For example, it's too high-level to say: We will create an online store with a shopping cart. It's clearer to state: We are responsible for the login, account creation, account management interface, shopping cart and confirmation emails.

Clearer estimates may reveal higher costs, but it's better to find that out while you can still control scope or expectations, rather than mid-project when you are reporting an overage.

5. DOUBLE-CHECK FOR COMMONLY OVERLOOKED ACTIVITIES

In the strain to consider every task, deliverable and bit of scope, it can be easy to overlook ancillary activities, such as meetings, edits on internal or client feedback and bug fixing. But these often-overlooked activities happen frequently during a project—and can frequently derail estimating efforts.

Though these tasks can have a huge impact on your estimate, it's difficult to gauge how long certain parts of the project will take. Feedback, for example, can range from "Change these two sentences" to "I don't like the concept, can you propose something else?" To handle this ambiguity, look at historical documents like past project reports and assess a percentage of the work rather than a specific amount of money or time.

6. INCLUDE THE ACCURACY OF THE ESTIMATE

Estimates are all guesses based on assumptions, but some guesses are more accurate than others. If the project involves using new technology, for example, then your estimate will be less accurate than if you're using a system the team already knows. In addition, many estimates are done too quickly due to time constraints; in those cases, the accuracy of estimates drastically diminishes.

It's crucial to communicate the accuracy of the estimate, meaning to specify by how much the amount given can vary. *A Guide to the Project Management Body of Knowledge (PMBOK® Guide)* provides the following guidelines:

1. Rough Order of Magnitude Estimate: –25 percent to +75 percent

2. Budget Estimate: −10 percent to +25 percent
3. Definitive Estimate: −5 percent to +10 percent

By communicating this information to your client, you set expectations and avoid surprising anyone when the estimate changes.

7. DON'T FORGET RISKS

This part may be tricky depending on how aware of risk management your team is. Often, the team will do a quick assessment, agree that it's a risky project and add more hours to the estimate.

However, that's not enough. Planning for your risk budget means using the registered risk and mitigation plans and accounting for the time needed to make those plans happen. For example, to prevent a technological constraint in a future phase of the project, you may plan to build a prototype. It would potentially avoid 200 hours of rework and would confirm the look and feel the team can obtain before the organization commits to the client. However, the prototype will still take 70 hours to build, and that effort needs to be taken into consideration when estimating the project.

Christian Bisson, PMP, is senior project manager at Mirum, Sainte-Julie, Quebec, Canada. He blogs at Voices on Project Management, ProjectManagement.com.

Cost-Benefit Paralysis

Prioritizing projects is straightforward when it comes down to ROI. Here's how to do it objectively when the budget's unclear.

Ibrahim Dani, PMP

At one organization I worked with, we were doing quite well in identifying potential projects, scoping them, and defining how these projects would be completed and what they would accomplish. What we lacked was an objective mechanism to rank these projects—especially when decision-makers were faced with shrewd sponsors pushing projects that might not necessarily warrant approval.

While projects in many companies are prioritized based on a cost-benefit analysis—particularly when there's a lack of a better framework—this approach wasn't practiced at this organization.

MORE MONEY, MORE PROBLEMS

For one thing, there was no comprehensive mechanism to measure the cost and benefits of project attributes and intended outcomes. Back then, a central projects group would authorize projects based on submissions by the project sponsor. And although the submissions included draft budgets, such budgets accounted for external costs only. Neither internal labor nor resourcing costs were included. Moreover, projects were funded from an organization-wide projects pool rather than the business units' annual budgets, meaning that few were rejected for lack of funds. If the sponsor could convince the central projects group that he or she needed this project, the custodians of the projects pool would finance it.

This increased the need for a project prioritization framework that didn't include monetary figures and, at the same time, one that could "objectify" subjective ratings obtained from different teams. Moreover, the framework needed to be strong enough so that the central projects group could easily push back projects supported by more influential sponsors.

GROUNDWORK FOR ORDER

After analyzing the situation and interviewing stakeholders, I devised a three-dimensional prioritization framework that emphasizes the business value of a project and highlights the nonfinancial attributes of its achievability:

- **Dimension A—value preservation:** Reflects the criticality of the project by identifying its importance and urgency in preserving the current business processes and value.

- **Dimension B—value addition:** Highlights new-business value the project will bring into the organization.

- **Dimension C—achievability:** Indicates how well the sponsor and project team understand the purpose and expected outcome of the project. This dimension also encompasses the project's risk profile and achievability in terms of available resources and technologies necessary for execution.

Each dimension is further divided into two sub-dimensions with different weights to increase the granularity of the scoring and reduce the subjectivity of the final score.

The figure below outlines the dimensions of the framework and shows their respective weights in parentheses.

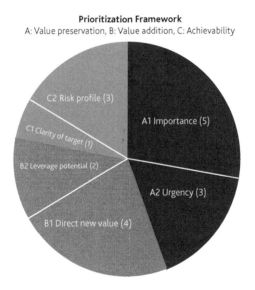

Prioritization Framework
A: Value preservation, B: Value addition, C: Achievability

C2 Risk profile (3)

C1 Clarity of target (1)

B2 Leverage potential (2)

B1 Direct new value (4)

A1 Importance (5)

A2 Urgency (3)

DRILLING DOWN

We developed a project prioritization group that, together with the project sponsor, identifies projects as either preserving the current business value (value preservation) or increasing the business value (value addition).

> When sponsors used this prioritization framework for the first time, many of them were surprised by the scores of certain projects. And they had to reluctantly accept the result and its rationale.

Unless the project is expected to deliver very high value in both dimensions, the project is categorized as either a value preservation (Dimension A) or value addition (Dimension B) project. This is to prevent projects from attracting high value unnecessarily by adding scores from both dimensions. After evaluating the project against either Dimension A or B, the project is evaluated against its achievability potential (Dimension C).

Then, the project prioritization group allocates a score of 0, 1 or 2 against each sub-dimension. This score is based on information collected by interviewing stakeholders and subject matter experts. The total score of each dimension is calculated, but all dimension scores are not added up. That is, each project has an A or B score and a C score. The higher value of A or B then sorts the projects, which are in turn sorted by the value of C. So for example, a project with a score of A8/C1 has a higher priority than a project with a score of A5/C8.

This type of weighted scoring provides the central projects group with better understanding of the criticality, value and achievability of the project. (See the sidebar The Prioritization Framework for details on weights and scoring.)

If a project attracts a zero score in both A and B dimensions, it will be rejected regardless of the score of

Dimension C. In other words, projects are not authorized only because they can be done—they are authorized if they need to be done.

THE BOTTOM LINE

Although most scoring is based on subjective opinion, the subjectivity of the total score is minimized by the granularity of the dimensions and the multiple scores obtained from different stakeholders. When sponsors used this prioritization framework for the first time, many of them were surprised by the scores of certain projects. And they had to reluctantly accept the result and its rationale.

Ibrahim Dani, PMP, is a program management consultant at FinXL IT Professional Services in Sydney, Australia.

Making the Leap

How to handle the challenges of moving to a large organization.

Amr Sadek, PMP

Whether you're a new project manager or an experienced one, moving from a small organization to a large one is challenging. It's not just that the company is bigger. It can also mean more layers of management, more dependencies and more complex processes. Below are four of the hurdles you might face, along with suggested solutions.

A DIVERSE MULTITUDE OF STAKEHOLDERS

In big organizations, you will usually need to work with stakeholders other than your direct team members. These stakeholders—such as R&D, marketing, sales, operations and support—may not all be housed in the same location, and they often don't share the same priorities.

You should use the stakeholder register and build a dedicated communication plan with different communication tools and techniques for different stakeholders.

Two-way communication is a must—this is no place for
the classic status email that sits unread in an inbox.

The steering committee is another helpful tool found
at some larger organizations. This committee allows you
to bring management and project sponsors together to
provide status updates and more easily receive the support needed to carry out the project.

UNCLEAR GOALS
Because of big firms' complex organizational structure,
the communication of goals from the top of the hier-
archy to the bottom is not always clear. This can cause
project team members to question the reason and the
value of what they're doing.

As a project manager, you must ask the right questions of management and the sponsors to understand the goals of the project. Communicating to your team how its project aligns to the organization's strategic goals will drive greater engagement and motivation for the team.

NON-CLASSICAL MODELS

Startups may be known for chasing big ideas, but big organizations do business in innovative ways. New delivery model ideas such as software as a service, cloud computing, platform as a service, infrastructure as a service, IT management as a service and others require up-to-date awareness of new standards and knowledge.

In addition, some large organizations employ revenue-sharing models with customers, where the two entities share the profits and losses. In these cases, you must adjust to a new goal that goes far beyond successful delivery of an agreed scope. You must ensure that the project will lead to more revenue for both your organization and the customer.

This requires a business mentality in addition to a project management mentality. It's essential that you understand the business case that the revenue-sharing model was built on. You also need to work closely with marketing teams, both in the organization and on the customer side, to better understand how the project is going to materialize in the customer program.

Normally in this model, the project manager is more relaxed on cost and scope control than in other projects, since the main focus is on building a platform that will bring future revenues. In these cases, adding to the scope or budget can often be justified if it would support the business case.

PROCESS AND MORE PROCESS

Heavy amounts of process could be one of the biggest sources of culture shock when joining a large organization. At first glance, these heavy processes might seem like a waste of time, but that's only the case if they're not used properly.

While a good project manager will spend time trying to learn all about the new company processes and follow them, a great one will start first by asking the right questions to quality and business efficiency teams. Your aim should be to understand the reasoning behind every process and what value it brings to the project. After a couple of successful deliverables, you might even be able to bring value by fine-tuning a process, depending on the project needs.

Amr Sadek, PMP, is a delivery manager for Africa and the Middle East at Gemalto, Dubai, United Arab Emirates.

Going Paperless

A government agency saved time and money with an e-construction process.

Kirk Steudle

In response to tight budgets and public demand for greater efficiency, the Department of Transportation in the U.S. state of Michigan is going paperless. Our goal is to collect, use and organize all data electronically.

We began in 2013 with a pilot project to use an e-construction process on four major highway contracts. The Michigan Department of Transportation (MDOT) was already using some paperless processes, such as electronic plans and electronic bidding. But in order to go completely paperless, other processes would have to be automated.

We had to make document management software accessible to all stakeholders, including contractors, engineers, suppliers, fabricators, testing personnel, inspectors and the Federal Highway Administration (FHWA). Field inspectors were provided with mobile devices so

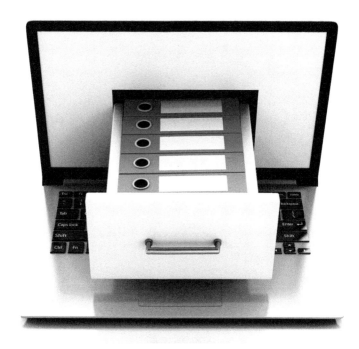

they could update electronic forms. Those forms could then be uploaded to a secure document management software program. The software program incorporated automated workflows to route documents to the correct reviewer or approver, to be approved electronically and routed to the next person. Everyone was required to use digital signatures.

SPEED BUMPS
The challenges were numerous. We had to upgrade technology at some field offices so their networks could operate at a sufficient speed. The use of digital

signatures raised legal concerns, such as compliance with state and federal regulations. Giving stakeholders access to the document management software meant overcoming IT concerns about the government network firewall. We also had to get the process formally approved by FHWA's Michigan Office. And we had to develop and communicate standards for electronic document files and a consistent naming convention to everyone involved with the projects.

Employees had to be trained on the new technology, so we developed a wiki site with instructions. Construction manuals were converted to e-books so they were more accessible and could be easily updated. Adding construction documentation was the logical next step in the paperless process, but it was only the beginning.

We began delivering contractual plans to contractors in a PDF format as they bid on projects electronically. The plans were supplemented by digital design data made available as part of digital Reference Information Documents (RID). The RID is posted pre-bid along with the electronically posted contractual plans. As part of a project to rebuild a portion of the I-96 freeway in the western suburbs of Detroit, contractors used this information to expedite their work, completing the US$150 million project in 167 days, compared to the original estimate of 261 days. Though the project also featured other innovations, the paperless aspect seems to have contributed to its speed.

This open and transparent document management system has had significant benefits for project delivery.

And even better results are just around the corner. Now, contractors rely on two-dimensional PDF plans and other digital design data from the RID to recreate three-dimensional models for their machine guidance. These recreated 3-D models may vary significantly from the original design intent, which can cause delays or problems during construction. So we are working to provide fully developed 3-D models as part of the RID.

THE BOTTOM LINE

This open and transparent document management system has had significant benefits for project delivery. The software is available to external partners on MDOT projects free of charge, as MDOT chose to incur the cost of an enterprise software license. Users can access project documentation on their desktop or laptop computer through a locally installed version of the software, or they can view documents from remote locations on mobile devices through a web portal or dedicated iPad application.

In addition to those time savings, a detailed analysis of one of the pilot projects, a US$25 million interchange construction project, revealed that the savings from paper, printing, postage, envelopes, labels and other fixed overhead costs totaled over US$300,000. The project eliminated 170,000 pieces of paper and saved a staggering 150,000 days of mail time. Projected out to the entire MDOT construction program, this equates to about US$12 million per year in savings in

[The program] is expected to eliminate about 7 million sheets of paper annually for MDOT's US$1 billion construction program.

measurable fixed-overhead costs for all stakeholders. It is expected to eliminate about 7 million sheets of paper annually for MDOT's US$1 billion construction program.

After the success of the pilot projects, MDOT began implementing e-construction across the entire construction program. Staff conducted training in every MDOT field office throughout the state, and statewide implementation began in the 2014 construction season.

Kirk Steudle is the director of the Michigan Department of Transportation, Lansing, Michigan, USA.

The Right Solution

How two collaboration tools solved
major project challenges.

Felix Meyer, PMP

Although collaboration tools alone don't guarantee successful projects, I have effectively addressed some of my larger project challenges by using two specific tools: a social network tool and a hosted collaborative project management solution.

A recent project to redesign an internal controls solution was extremely challenging from a communications perspective. There were more than 2,500 users in a variety of divisions and locations whom I would email periodically with precise timelines and instructions. Through informal sessions with users, I found out that many people did not read the emails. Even fewer asked questions about things they did not understand.

Clearly, my messages were getting lost in the slew of other emails being received in the course of daily work.

I turned the situation around by implementing a project-specific collaboration group in Yammer, a social

networking tool our company uses. I immediately noticed a higher level of attention to my messages for three reasons:

1. **Concentration of information.** Users did not have to search for emails relating to my subject. Instead, when they had a moment, they could easily browse posts for the pertinent information. To direct users to this page, I would stress during calls and training sessions that they should check the collaboration page as a one-stop shop for any new posts, training material, links to videos and project information.

2. **Ease of search.** Information could be found quickly because it was hashtagged. Though this required me to earmark certain posts, it created a structured approach to finding specific information.

3. **Information sharing.** Not only could I follow up easily with the entire community when users had questions, but I even saw that the community was contributing answers, providing tips and sharing best practices that peers could benefit from.

Although I did have to put in a bit of extra effort to onboard the users and review the consistency of the posts, the payoff was worth it: Users got a clear message about the project without any additional effort on their part.

AN EASIER WAY

During my last project, the upgrade of a global treasury management solution, I realized the time I spent chasing project team members to provide me status updates on issues and work packages was distracting me from managing other parts of the project. In addition, I saw that granting access to my project sheets to people outside our organization so they could update them imposed a burden on my information systems department.

Although I did have to put in a bit of extra effort to onboard the users and review the consistency of the posts, the payoff was worth it: Users got a clear message about the project without any additional effort on their part.

Turning to a hosted collaborative project management solution (over 150 listed are on Wikipedia), I quickly gained the following benefits with minimal configuration:

1. **Content restriction:** My new tool enabled me to assign permission to update documents at the issue, task or even field level. Additionally, when users modified content, the tool would email me about the records that had been modified.

2. **Resource empowerment:** By assigning the ownership of issues and work packages to the project team and configuring a weekly reminder process that reminded owners to update their status (access to the solution was from any web or mobile device), I no longer had to chase users down. Instead, users became empowered to deliver status updates and comments without much additional effort.

3. **Status summary reports:** The collaboration tool would automatically send senior stakeholders a weekly project update. Not only did this save me time, it also brought my stakeholders closer to the ongoing status of the project.

Clearly, to achieve these benefits, minimal configuration was required (setting permissions, configuring emails, establishing frequency of reminders, configuring reports). But by pushing some of the work to its source, I could spend more time analyzing the results and trying to manage the issues in the project.

As all projects have unique challenges, finding the right collaboration tools to assist you can require a time investment and luck. However, once an appropriate tool is found, it won't be hard to see the benefit that technology will bring to you and your stakeholders.

Felix Meyer, PMP, is a project manager and assistant vice president at ABB Information Systems, Zurich, Switzerland.

Measuring Delay

Introducing a "pseudo resource"—Delay—can clarify your project schedule.

Sriram Rajagopalan, PMI-ACP, PMI-RMP, PMI-SP, PMP

Project managers often face one major question from stakeholders: "Is your project on schedule?"

Schedule slips are a particular concern in healthcare marketing. In the U.S., healthcare organizations' marketing deliverables—including print or online advertisements, surveys and reports—must go through an intense review by a regulatory board. This board, made up of medical, legal and regulatory members, reviews the content and functionality prior to its submission to the Food and Drug Administration for approval to distribute. Projects may experience unexpected delays because of these external stakeholders. So how can project managers evaluate the cost of these delays and proactively manage resource productivity?

INTRODUCING A PSEUDO RESOURCE

I imagine the source of the delay as a "pseudo resource"—a fictitious person—named Delay. Anytime there is an unanticipated regulatory delay, instead of updating the duration of the review task, I introduce a new task, called delay. I list the cause and duration of the delay and assign the task to the Delay pseudo resource. This approach ensures that any rebaselining of the project schedule doesn't extend the original review

> Anytime there is an unanticipated regulatory delay, instead of updating the duration of the review task, I introduce a new task, called delay.

task, indicating inefficient client management skills on the project manager's part.

BENEFITS OF DELAY AS A RESOURCE

When such delay tasks are introduced in the work breakdown structure, the project manager can generate reports that measure the difference between actual finish and baseline finish days in the network diagram, and then subtract the duration associated with the delays. This allows the project manager to manage client expectations during the delay cycle and reset the expectations for the new finish date. Simultaneously, the project manager can reassign resources earlier during the delay period to other projects, with requests for them to return when tasks are coming out of the delay cycle. Neither fast-tracking nor crashing is required—just proactive planning to minimize the impact of resource changes.

For the project management office (PMO), the benefits are even greater. By computing the percentage of slip with the delays over the project duration, we can figure out how much the delay impacted the project. For example, imagine the baseline finish date originally was on 15 May 2015, with a project duration of 60 days. The actual finish was 2 June 2015, including a five-day regulatory review associated with the Delay pseudo resource. The schedule slipped by 11 business days. The cost of delay to the project is 18 percent (11/60). On the other hand, by using this approach factoring in the five-day delay, the schedule slipped by six days (11-5), and the cost of delay is only 10 percent (6/60).

In other words, Cost of Delay (%) = (Actual Finish − Baseline Finish − Delay Duration) / (Total Project Duration).

LOOK FOR PATTERNS

By seeing patterns—whether delays arise from a particular type of project or from regulatory reviews, specific project managers or team members—the PMO can hold early lessons-learned sessions. In addition, the report can be used to see how many projects are slipping, giving indications on inefficient resource management practices, ambiguous tasks and roles creating unnecessary productivity loss, and opportunities for process enhancements. Using integrated change control, the impact of these delay costs can be identified and mitigated by proper risk management discipline.

Sriram Rajagopalan, PMI-ACP, PMI-RMP, PMI-SP, PMP, is vice president of the program management office (PMO) at Physicians Interactive, Reading, Massachusetts, USA and founder of Agile Training Champions.

The 20-Percent Solution

How to stop playing games with your project schedule.

Ronald B. Smith, PMP

Most recently baselined project plans are inaccurate because they have unrealistic start dates, finish dates, work hours, costs and/or durations. Poor estimating during the planning phase is a big contributor to project failures.

However, project managers can build more accuracy and credibility into their project plans by incorporating the 20-percent solution into three areas.

REALISTIC SCHEDULES

No one is available to work on projects 100 percent of his or her time—people take breaks, attend meetings, get stuck in traffic and so on. Therefore, you should make the assumption a resource is unavailable 20 percent of the time and available 80 percent. If a resource is available only half-time for a project, set the maximum units of availability at 40 percent.

Also remember to include holidays, plant shutdowns, training and individual resource vacations when setting up your project's schedule.

BUFFER PROTECTION

No plan ever runs according to schedule. Some tasks will come in late, so you need some wiggle room. A good idea is to add a buffer task at the end of selected

No plan ever runs according to schedule. Some tasks will come in late, so you need some wiggle room.

phases (for example, phases involving new technology that your team has limited or no experience using) or to extend the project's summary end date for that phase by 20 percent from its original duration. For example, if the original phase duration is 100 days, extend it to 120 days.

If you don't end up using the entire buffer, reduce the buffer's duration time to get an accurate project completion date. If you don't use any of the buffer, delete or inactivate it (remove the values from your rolled-up schedule). In this situation, I recommend inactivating the task so it is saved for historical reasons and can be reactivated later if needed for an emergency.

MANAGING RISKS

Since organizations usually don't spend enough time on risk management, contingency funds totaling 20 percent of the total budget should be set up for each project.

There are two types of risks. Known unknowns are identified at the beginning of the project, and unknown unknowns are identified during the execution of the project. Set up contingency funds of 10 percent of the budget for each of these risk categories. These safety margins should obviate the need for padding task estimates (probably the worst habit a project manager can develop) and similar games, and help to produce an honest project plan that will get stakeholder buy-in.

Following these three tips should improve your project plan's credibility and performance. If you discover over time and through lessons learned that the 20-percent figure is not appropriate for your organization, adjust to what works best (for example, 17.5 percent or 25 percent).

Ronald B. Smith, PMP, is recently retired from IBM Global Services and now teaches project management to technical graduate students at the University of Houston, Houston, Texas, USA.

Part 3

Strategic and Business Management

In today's business environment, a project manager cannot focus solely on the deliverables of his or her projects. In order to make sure the project delivers business value, the practitioner must have knowledge of and expertise in the industry and organization. He or she needs to know the strategic alignment of the project, understand finances, be able to speak the language of executives, and know the value of project management in the global economy.

A frequent project in the world of IT is to create or modify an enterprise resource planning (ERP) system. A column writer outlines three steps to ensure that the ERP is aligned with organizational strategy.

How do you measure success? One article cites research and a construction-industry case study to spell out the factors. Another article tells how you can delve into customer satisfaction surveys to identify trends in customer priorities and plan for future success.

If you like the idea of agile approaches to project management bringing more business value to your organization but you are in a mature, regulated industry like defense or pharmaceuticals, learn how your company can still benefit from an agile-based approach.

Being competent in strategic and business management, as well as technical skills and leadership skills, will make you a more complete project manager and increase your value in the marketplace.

Survey Says

How reliable are your portfolio's customer satisfaction surveys?

Chris D'Ascenzo, DBA, PgMP, PfMP

Using customer satisfaction surveys in a portfolio of IT projects and programs presents complex challenges. Portfolio managers must balance strategic objectives against external customers' demands spelled out in survey results. And in large organizations, portfolio managers have to align portfolios to strategies that serve different customer cultures.

But one of the biggest challenges is even more fundamental: determining how useful these surveys are and finding ways to improve them.

As an executive in the national security and defense industry, I once led a portfolio containing over 100 projects, task orders and program elements, and more than 1,000 IT employees. With so many factors, I began to realize that implementing a customer satisfaction discipline was necessary to assess how our customers saw us. But I knew it was not sufficient to gauge customer affinity or to make investment decisions. Favorable customer satisfaction doesn't tend to be a strong predictor of retaining customers in the face of factors like IT service delivery model efficiencies, migration to cloud architectures and value pricing.

For four years, my portfolio team conducted detailed customer satisfaction surveys addressing responsiveness, teamwork, conflict resolution, back-office support, agility and overall satisfaction. We also developed a value measurement framework to add context to the customer satisfaction data-collection process. We implemented guidelines on tangible and intangible benefits recognition, expected values of benefits on a project or program basis, and a host of approaches for customer engagement and analysis.

This customer satisfaction survey discipline worked. Still, our ability to assume that we would garner new business or retain long-term contracts during a market downturn could not depend on survey data alone. While it provided good feedback, it did not yield a reliable leading indicator of repeat business.

So my organization adopted a more strategic use of the customer satisfaction information. To shape the portfolio, we began to look beyond the data and identified potential gaps in our competitive differentiation by using the satisfaction metrics themselves.

For example, the surveys showed that although clients gave us excellent ratings in the majority of the portfolio accounts, it was getting cheaper for them to switch to alternative IT services suppliers. This prompted us to evaluate more aggressive and creative pricing and staffing solutions. Additionally, I noticed over time that several clients gave us excellent overall satisfaction ratings, but their emphasis on back-office support rose steadily as client budgets became more aggressive. Ignoring this trend despite excellent customer satisfaction scores would take the edge off our competitive value proposition going forward.

Looking beyond the obvious customer satisfaction data also allowed us to identify trends in customer priorities. These trends could be determined from doing a regression analysis on the satisfaction data. In several instances, subtle shifts in customer strategic emphasis, like teleworking and social media infrastructure evolution, were detectable—just enough to help us in developing counter strategies to shape the portfolio and ward off competition.

In the case of customer satisfaction measurement, we learned valuable lessons about collecting data and looking beyond it. I continue to try to find more leading indicators of portfolio performance.

Chris D'Ascenzo, DBA, PgMP, PfMP, is founder of Ascendt Group LLC, Green Lane, Pennsylvania, USA. He can be reached at chris@ascendtgroup.com.

Blame Game

Look to your organization's strategy and processes to prevent project failure.

Grace Willis, PMP

Project managers often take the fall for failures, even though a project consists of many working parts. But the real culprit is often a lack of strategy and processes to support a project's successful delivery.

In my career, I have not seen executives realize, much less acknowledge, the inherent bond among strategy, process and projects. Instead, I have been assigned to projects that were incomplete ideas.

It often happens like this: Something tied to operations is not working well. A decision-maker opts to try to solve the problem with a project. A project manager is hired, a staff member is assigned to be the project manager or a software developer is promoted to the role. A third-party vendor—regardless of qualifications—is engaged. No one checks to see if there is a master services agreement with a similar vendor somewhere else in the organization. Team members are drafted to the

project regardless of skill level, commitment and availability. The team is reluctant to voice concerns to the decision-maker.

The project begins and goes wrong immediately: Tasks are delayed, and team members begin to skip meetings and conference calls—or worse, they attend but are mentally absent. Eventually, the vendor collects money for a bad product or service, and the project manager is blamed.

More than a project manager failure, this fiasco is due to a lack of strategy and process.

No project should ever make it past the proposal stage without being aligned to a corporate strategy. Corporate strategy is a well-thought-out directive of where the organization is headed in order to serve its market. The initiatives required in order to put this strategy into effect are then articulated and delegated. A corporate strategy is essential before any potential projects are born, and strategy drives not only the projects but also their scope and timing.

Next, before the project begins, a feasibility analysis should result in identification of existing processes. Does the organization even have processes? If so, how do they potentially support or hinder the project? What are the gaps? If there are existing gaps that would hinder progress, can they be addressed?

A process analysis needs to be performed by a Six Sigma expert. Process analysis is critical to successful project implementation as it allows for a conscientious and comprehensive review of the infrastructure in place that transcends relevant groups, like business

No project should ever make it past the proposal stage without being aligned to a corporate strategy.

and IT. Variations across internal groups and regional and international locations should also be taken into consideration if this is an enterprise-wide project. The practicality and likelihood of successfully bridging these process gaps pre-launch need to be identified, as these gaps represent risk.

Then of course, there is the real work involved. Get processes on track before even thinking about project kickoff. It is amazing to me that many projects get off the ground, even with a feasibility study having purportedly been conducted, when there was no consideration of either strategy or process.

Strategy, process and projects are inextricably interwoven. Ignore any one of these elements, and you have set yourself up for failure. Only by respecting these ties that bind can you avert blame and your organization avoid having its projects join the large percentage of projects that fail to meet their objectives, are delivered late, exceed their budgets or get scrapped altogether.

Grace Willis, PMP, is a freelance consultant/agile coach within the continental USA.

The Path to Enlightenment

Many organizations are far from reaching project, program and portfolio management nirvana. But they still can help grow the profession.

Paul C. Dinsmore, PMP, PMI Fellow

Our profession has been in constant mutation since the dawn of modern project management in the 1950s. From its most simplistic form of dealing with a single project to running complex programs in ever-changing environments like high-tech space exploration, the profession of project management has broadened considerably. Project, program and portfolio managers require a rock-solid set of policies, structure, guidelines and procedures to herd the plethora of projects that often butt heads at stampede-like pace to meet desired goals.

What looms next on the horizon? Is there no end to the rampant scope creep assailing the profession? What will project management eventually encompass?

Is there no end to the rampant scope creep assailing the profession?

WHERE WE ARE NOW
Here are some of the ways projects are currently handled in organizations:

1. **Laissez Faire** ("let them do as they choose"). Projects are carried out as required using intuitive approaches or methodologies that vary from one initiative to another. Nobody knows how many projects are underway in the organization or their statuses.

2. **Departmental.** Each department or group develops methodology and practices appropriate for it. No cross-fertilization exists with other departments.

3. **Project Management Offices, or PMOs.** Some orga-
    nizations have one PMO, while others have multiple
    at different levels in different regions. They sometimes
    are connected, yet often operate independently.

4. **Corporate-Level PMO** (top-down oversight). Here,
    a chief project officer, corporate PMO or strategic
    PMO cares for the implementation of strategic proj-
    ects and the overall project management practice in
    the organization, including portfolio management.

5. **Enterprise Project Governance.** This all-encom-
    passing organizational approach involves key play-
    ers, including board members, executives, portfolio
    managers, PMO managers and project managers.
    It aims to ensure the alignment of the corporate
    portfolio and its programs and projects with overall
    strategy. Actions are taken proactively to confirm
    that everything stays on track to ultimately create
    value for the organization.

This last approach is designed to meet a crying need:
to deal intelligently and efficiently with the numerous
projects and programs demanded by the marketplace,
and with evolving technology, stakeholders, regulatory
agencies and the quest to innovate. Organizations are
under greater pressure to do all this with limited resources and at record-making speed.

REACHING ENLIGHTENMENT

Assuming the trend continues toward broader views
for managing projects across organizations, where
might the quest for a comprehensive holistic view
lead? Is there another level—some sort of project management nirvana, a glorious stage of organizational
enlightenment?

Until such enlightenment, the five approaches listed above all could use an upgrade. Here's how to boost project management effectiveness in each:

- **Laissez faire** may fare well—provided projects are few in number and "hero" project managers are at the helm. Other circumstances call for more structure and process, through a PMO perhaps, to increase the organization's project management maturity.

- The **departmental** way of managing projects is effective within certain organizational microcosms, such as IT and engineering, where departmental PMOs are helpful in guaranteeing best practices. To be more effective, the departments must reach out to other areas in the organization to consolidate common practices and create a broad project management culture.

- **PMOs** are the stanchions for project management methodology and support in organizations. In terms of authority and responsibility, however, their postures vary from the timid to the proud and powerful. But power wielded by a PMO is less important than its effectiveness in supporting and facilitating projects to meet organizational goals. Effective PMOs evolve constantly and strive to spread best practices across the organization.

- The **corporate-level PMO** views projects strategically as they are selected, evolve and are brought to fruition. Because this type of PMO resides in the upper echelons of an organization, it has access to decision-makers and can greatly increase overall project management effectiveness through portfolio management, standardization of methodologies, acquisition of technologies and providing training on a corporate-wide basis.

* **Enterprise project governance,** in theory, stands the best chance of coming close to project management enlightenment. The challenge involves overcoming the cultural hurdles and turf battles that stand in the way. But it will take persistence, top-level support and long-range strategies.

Imagine it: full-fledged project management nirvana, where all stakeholders experience a state of complete fulfillment and joy.

It might not be fully attainable, but it's an admirable dream to pursue. Project professionals can make giant steps in that direction no matter what approach they currently use. The destination isn't really as important as the professional journey toward the goal. That journey surely will spawn improved practices as the profession evolves to improve results at the portfolio level.

Paul C. Dinsmore, PMP, PMI Fellow, is partner at DC - DinsmoreCompass, a project and change management consultancy based in Rio de Janeiro, Brazil. He is the co-author of *Enterprise Project Governance*.

Building Blocks

Research into successful projects reveals
six underlying factors.

Terry Williams, PMP

For 20 years I have been on a mission to understand how projects behave, what we can learn from them and how we can better manage them.

I thought it would be refreshing to look into why projects succeed rather than why they fail. But I faced two obstacles. First, "project success" is a multidimensional measure that means different things to different people. For example, the Sydney Opera House could now be deemed a success, yet it was completed six years behind schedule and at double the original cost. Second, there has been little research into the causal chains that lead to the success.

A CASE STUDY

My work led me to undertake a case study of the delivery of projects by Sewell Group in Hull, England between 2008 and 2013. The projects were part of two government programs in health and education—the

One of Sewell's projects:
Wilberforce Health
Centre in Hull, England

National Health Service Local Improvement Finance Trust Programme and the Building Schools for the Future Programme.

Sewell's delivery of the projects, equating to £500 million of new and improved public facilities in the city of Hull, was generally considered excellent. But I wanted to explore whether the projects were regarded as successful due to positive feelings created from significant regeneration investment in a concentrated area, or if Sewell had, in fact, delivered project excellence.

My research showed that the firm not only applied the traditional criteria of a well-run project (time, cost and quality), it also went much further, aiming to leave a legacy and address more intangible criteria such as customer satisfaction, user and community engagement, and empathy.

In short, it was a success. But what exactly led to that success?

SIX SUCCESS FACTORS

As part of my research, we conducted workshops with project teams and managers to draw up causal maps of effect to try to uncover the chains of causality. That work led to the revelation of these six root causal areas for the projects' success:

Company culture—Sewell Group has a strong internal culture of delivering on promises and high leadership skills throughout the organization as a result of a less layered management structure.

The single team—The organization created a superior product through a single-team approach from the outset. The collaboration included everyone involved in the project development and delivery—client, subcontractors, designers, facilities management, etc.

Project setup—Identifying stakeholders and decision makers early, and engaging with these groups, helped the team manage expectations and led to better project setup. Stakeholders bought into the process and timelines, and users and clients understood the final result before it came. The thorough project setup also meant there were fewer changes as the project proceeded, and many issues and risks could be aired and avoided rather than retrospectively addressed.

Customer satisfaction—This was achieved through a consistent partnership and engagement between Sewell and the customer throughout the project. It led to a better functioning product, fewer disputes and more promises that were delivered.

Subcontractors—A great deal of effort was put into relationships with subcontractors. The teams had delivery and quality in mind, not just cheapest price. The subcontractors were involved in the bid, producing a feeling of "if we win it, you win it" and partnership, which helped build shared goals between Sewell and the subcontractors, leading to better performance.

Post-handover—The project is not complete at building handover. Understanding this is an important element in the performance of construction projects. Sewell's facilities management division had long-term maintenance responsibility for the buildings it designed and built. Because of this, Sewell actually feels like the end user. This "soft landing" results in better project outcomes and service.

More details on this research can be found in the paper "Identifying Success Factors in Construction Projects—A Case Study," which appeared in *Project Management Journal*.

Terry Williams, PMP, was Dean of Hull University Business School, England, and is now leading risk research at the university.

Trying Agile on for Size

Even mature industries can benefit from an iterative approach.

Jennifer Kaniecki MacNeil, PMI-ACP, PMP

For project managers working in mature, regulated industries such as defense or pharmaceuticals, the prospect of changing to an agile-based approach for project delivery may seem daunting. Project governance in these industries has achieved a level of maturity and success with a reliance on the traditional waterfall method. However, the ability to demonstrate value and calculate return on investment often lags project completion, particularly for multidiscipline and multiyear projects. Given the increased pressures on project teams to not just deliver value, but to deliver it early and often, it might be time to consider a change.

Seven years ago, when I began working in information technology for Bechtel Plant Machinery Inc. in support of the Naval Nuclear Propulsion Program, the agile approach was often discussed but not used. However, by introducing the basic principles of agile, with an iterative approach and self-organizing teams, several of

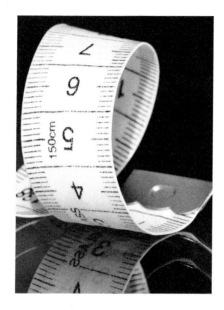

our project managers were able to lay the foundation for change.

Because agile is a philosophy, we didn't have to focus on the mechanics of introducing a new project methodology and all that it entails (e.g., new governance). Instead, we partnered our project teams and project customers in order to decompose a project into iterations, each of which had well-defined value propositions. This change in philosophy helped our project teams in three important ways:

STRENGTHENED RELATIONSHIPS

Prioritizing high-value items across and within iterations ensures the project customer and team are aligned and working toward the same goals, with a focus on delivering value in the near term. Delivering at more frequent intervals enables the project customer to have more consistent involvement with the project team and increased opportunities to provide input. With more frequent interaction, issues can be identified and resolved earlier to lower the project risk.

INCREASED TEAM MORALE

With agile, project teams are not looking down a long project timeline toward handoffs and stages to keep the water falling on a project. Teams realize a sense of accomplishment with each iteration. They witness their impact on value when earlier return-on-investment calculations can be made. Confidence in the team's ability to deliver is increased for not just the team but the project customer.

IMPROVED PLANNING AND EXECUTION

As iterations are completed, the successes and challenges can be applied to future iterations to improve the project team's delivery capability. Lessons learned don't wait for project completion, but can be incorporated throughout the project. As teams understand what they can deliver in an iteration, they can better estimate future iterations.

As the pressure to deliver value early and often increases, project teams need to focus on the value proposition as part of project planning. Incorporating agile principles, particularly focusing on an iterative approach, enhances project delivery success and enables project teams to deliver a steady flow of value.

Jennifer Kaniecki MacNeil, PMI-ACP, PMP, is an adviser in program management at Bechtel Plant Machinery Inc., Pittsburgh, Pennsylvania, USA.

Becoming Agile

One organization's experience with adopting agile practices proves instructive— and profitable.

Michal Raczka, MBA, PMI-ACP, PMP

In 2011, our organization, e-commerce company Allegro Group, realized it needed a way to quickly react to changes in the market. Our waterfall process was not allowing us to do that, so we started making our way toward agility. The problems that cropped up and the lessons we learned on the way can help other organizations embarking on the same journey.

We started with a pilot project—our first Scrum team. We soon experienced the "two clocks issue," in which the Scrum team was moving quickly, but the entire organization was not ready to make the change. Part of the problem was that we were unable to communicate well. Years of living in caves of specialization on different floors left us unaccustomed to communicating face-to-face with everyone—something that agile requires.

What's more, although we said we were working in sprints, our sprints were just mini-waterfalls, and we

struggled to think in terms of user value. Another problem was the availability of our first Scrum team members. Despite the agreement that our entire team would be dedicated full-time to the project, we faced a stream of requests for help with other work.

Nevertheless, in spite of the pilot project's challenges, management decided that agile should go company-wide. We found an experienced agile coach and started training all levels of the company. We began moving employees from silos to teams. Within two days everybody changed seats, floors—even buildings. Businesspeople now sat with IT people. This presented a huge administration challenge, but there were no longer problems with communication or availability of team members.

PMO CHALLENGE

Meanwhile, I faced the challenge of implementing a new agile process in the project management office (PMO). My method was to suspend all rules and to give teams the freedom to find creative solutions. Every project manager was able to manage the project using his or her own style—the only requirement was to use the agile approach. After one year, we agreed on one common process, which we call the "agile project management process." It is consistent with Scrum but modified for the strong usage of project management.

During the transition, my organization realized why it is so hard to achieve high agility. It is not about doing agile; it is about being agile. At the beginning we were focused on the mechanics of Scrum/agile. But this accounts for only 20 percent of the success—the other 80 percent pertains to culture and people. We had to adjust our thinking to be open to change, look for quick feedback and act on it, and adapt to new situations.

Our journey is not over. Still, we have seen remarkable success using agile: shorter time to market, close cooperation between business and IT, and more employee satisfaction.

Michal Raczka, MBA, PMI-ACP, PMP, is IT Director at Naspers Group/Allegro Group, Poland.

Taking Measures

How to assess your organization's agility transformation program.

Mustafa Dülgerler, MBA, PMP

Organizations are spending significant amounts of time and money trying to improve their agility. But if project practitioners don't properly measure the results of these transformation programs, they'll never know whether or not they succeeded.

Agility is the ability of an organization to sense change in its environment and respond quickly and appropriately, according to PMI's *Pulse of the Profession®: Capturing the Value of Project Management Through Organizational Agility*. Because changes around us never stop, project managers have to closely monitor organizational agility programs. The measurement process can be broken down into to three phases—before the agility transformation program, during it and after. A number of quantitative and qualitative measurements can be used, in addition to the ones specific to your industry:

QUANTITATIVE METHODS

Return on agility ratios. These are ratios of the after-agile to before-agile conditions. Examples include how product delivery time, IT expenses and operational expenses changed as a result of the agility program.

Key performance indicators (KPIs). KPIs to measure agility progress could include number of units sold, length of production cycle or number of people trained. The best practice is to rank KPIs from different dimensions, such as priority and criticality.

In the decision-making process, the KPIs can be evaluated individually. However, it is better to consider them in correlation with the other KPIs. For instance, an organization could look at whether employees who've undergone the training actually sell more units.

Organizations should never consider the selected KPIs as a static list, because business requirements, customer demands and more will change over time. Hence, the chosen KPIs should be reviewed regularly to ensure their validity, priority and necessity. In some cases, additional KPIs will need to be introduced.

Balanced scorecard (BSC). A BSC can measure performance from four angles: customer, financial, internal business processes, and learning and growth. Using a BSC to identify the gaps in the current organizational processes and improving them will enhance the speed of achieving organizational strategies, and also improve the level of organizational agility.

QUALITATIVE METHODS

Two main qualitative methods can measure the adoption of the new agile culture in an organization:

Interviews. These can generate both breadth and depth of information about a topic. They can lead to better understanding and rapport with the interviewees in comparison to other methods such as questionnaires. Because the interviews are dynamic, interviewees can further clarify if the question is unclear to them; similarly, the interviewer can ask further questions to better understand the interviewee's feedback.

> **Project managers have a great responsibility to manage agility transformations successfully, and this is only possible with the right monitoring and controlling tools and techniques.**

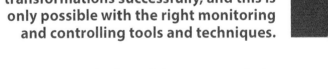

However, this method may fail to overcome the issue of bias. Interviewees may not want to reveal what they actually think about the change. Defining the target audience for interviews is also generally a challenge, as interviewing the entire organization is expensive and time-consuming. Therefore, the right audience should be selected, and it should include the key decision-makers and employees.

Surveys and questionnaires. These techniques will help you access and get feedback from a larger audience, but they require a deeper analysis to formulate questions, which must be as precise as possible.

Project managers have a great responsibility to manage agility transformations successfully, and this is only possible with the right monitoring and controlling tools and techniques. Only by properly measuring can we bring our organizations to a stage where they not only adopt change, but also drive change.

Mustafa Dülgerler, MBA, PMP, is a senior enterprise architect at National Bank of Abu Dhabi, Abu Dhabi, United Arab Emirates. He can be reached at mdulgerler@gmail.com.

Smooth Operator

How to use your project management skills in operations.

Deepa Gandhavalli Ramaniah, PMP

Although an operation is completely different from a project, many project managers find themselves in roles involving operations. The good news is the jobs involve a considerable overlap in skills.

Consider a business operation such as production support, design maintenance or remediation. Here, operations managers focus on executing, monitoring and controlling the business operations so that business goals are achieved. This will sound familiar to project managers, who execute, monitor and control a project's process groups.

Here are three of the most important project management skills needed if you find yourself in operations management:

COMMUNICATION
As a liaison to multiple stakeholders, an operations manager needs to plan communications by identifying

all the required stakeholders, then working out the mode and frequency of communication for each of them. For example, an operations manager handling a production support team needs to communicate the list of prioritized activities to the operations team, relate the progress of tickets or requests to customers, and keep senior management informed of operational activities.

Operations managers also need to proactively identify and communicate any potential overdue tasks to the required stakeholders, as well as escalate any non-compliance to service level agreements according to the organization's escalation policies and procedures. Once, while managing a production support team, I handled a highly escalated customer ticket as a small-scale project. Since the ticket had a huge impact on the production environment, the customer insisted on getting an immediate fix or patch. I arranged a quick meeting of the operations team to make sure we understood the issue, its root cause and the impact. When we were unable to identify a temporary fix, we knew we would have to develop a permanent one and release a patch. Considering the customer's business impact, I met with the senior management stakeholders immediately, summarized the issue and explained that it should be handled as a mini project. My communications skills, honed while managing projects, were a great asset at this point.

NEGOTIATION AND INFLUENCING

When an operations manager handles a high-severity customer request or a production ticket, he or she might have to use negotiation and influencing skills to acquire highly skilled technical resources from a project team. Negotiation may also be required to explain to the customer about the complexity of tickets being handled by the operations team and buy additional time, if required. At times, the operations manager might even have to negotiate with and influence his or her team members to get tasks done.

In my operations mini-project, the next step after communicating was to devise a plan and negotiate with senior executives to create a "tiger team" of different resources, such as an architect who could propose a permanent fix, a designer who could implement, a configuration manager who could build the code and develop a patch, and a lead tester who could deploy the patch and test all possible scenarios, with the architect's assistance. But because those people were already assigned to projects, I had to negotiate with project managers. To create a win-win situation, I had earlier negotiated with senior executives that this escalation would be the highest priority, and any other program or project would have to be deprioritized. This meant project managers willingly lent the resources required for the tiger team.

LEADERSHIP

An operations manager must direct, facilitate, coach and lead teams to handle daily operations. He or she should be aware of the competencies possessed by the team and assign tasks accordingly. He or she also must motivate team members through continuous appreciation and recognition.

The operations manager should possess excellent problem-solving and decision-making skills. For instance, when a production problem arises, an operations manager should have a complete understanding of the problem's context, impact and consequences before making a decision on the timeline for resolution. It is also a good practice to meet with the operations team to get its buy-in on the timeline before committing to the customer.

It's common for operational team members to disagree on issues or solutions to problems. The operations manager must take the lead, bring the team members together, get their thoughts, analyze pros and cons of each member's proposal and identify the best-fit solution. It is the operations manager's responsibility to create a problem-solving environment and manage conflict.

Returning to my example: Once the team was formed through negotiation and influencing, we held a brief meeting to explain the background, what was

It is the operations manager's responsibility to create a problem-solving environment and manage conflict.

expected from each resource, the project deadlines and so on. As operations manager, I made sure the team had all the required resources, such as hardware and software, to execute the project. I directed the lead tester to get involved during the implementation phase itself, so he could prepare the test cases and get them reviewed by the architect before the patch got delivered to him for testing. I worked to ensure the tiger team was constantly motivated and empowered to fix the issue by the deadline.

But at one point, two members of the team got into a serious argument over an error. I called them to a meeting and, using my interpersonal skills, explained that we were not there to blame but to get the patch to the customer by the deadline. I persuaded them to shake hands and proceed with the next phase. After successful testing of the patch, we were able to deliver it to the customer as planned. Finally, I arranged a meeting with the tiger team and senior executives and made sure the team was recognized for its work.

Deepa Gandhavalli Ramaniah, PMP, is senior associate—projects at Cognizant Technology Solutions, Chennai, India.

Reversing the Trend

Three steps to ensure your next enterprise resource planning (ERP) implementation project aligns with organizational strategy.

Raed M. Skaf, PMP, PgMP

Many organizations try to implement enterprise resource planning (ERP) to improve their business workflow. Unfortunately, 54 percent of ERP implementation projects took longer than expected and 56 percent exceeded budget, according to research from Panorama Consulting Group. What's more, 50 percent of ERP implementation projects realize less than half of the expected benefits.

The causes of failure aren't just technical—they're managerial slip-ups. For example, one of the root causes of failure is not considering changes to existing business processes, the cost of subject-matter experts (SMEs) or the cost of infrastructure in estimates. Resistance to change is another obstacle often not considered.

As organizations become increasingly mature in project management, the failure percentage should

decrease. Project professionals and the executive suite must improve communication of organizational strategy.

To start, project managers should paint the full picture of ERP project execution to executive stakeholders in order to prevent unwanted surprises and risks, and avoid execution failure. This includes analyzing the current information system's capability, business processes and future business needs—as well as considering the possible benefits or business strategies that can be achieved.

In addition, these factors support a successful ERP project:

- **Business case**—to justify project existence and requirements

- **Top management commitment**—to support the project from initiation to full implementation of the ERP software

- **Project management**—to govern the project, deliver quality products, monitor progress and feedback, and anticipate and mitigate risks

- **Change management**—to involve people from the field to avoid resistance to change

- **Training**—to guide all levels in the project group and provide special courses for some users when necessary

- **SMEs**—to facilitate successful implementation when a new generation of technology is involved (includes vendor support)

This three-step process can support the alignment between strategy and project execution:

Step 1: Strategic environment and assumptions assessment. Top management must assess the current and future situation in which the organization will operate. This information will impact the company's choice of business strategies and objectives. Achieve this by leveraging a group setting to ask open-ended questions about current issues affecting the organization, such as: What are our highest-priority problems that need to be tackled first? Who should be the project sponsor? Where are the as-is processes, and how we can capture the point of failures and convert to to-be processes? Agree on actions to be taken to overcome these issues.

Step 2: Strategic planning. Understanding the strategic environment and assumptions helps senior leaders establish organizational objectives. This includes the set of ideas that, when fully developed, will contribute to the realization of the objectives.

Step 3: Portfolio planning. ERP implementation projects should be grouped with business process reengineering projects, training projects for end-users and administrators, and communication management projects in an overall portfolio. This ensures ERP projects take high priority, as well as helps show their ROI. It ensures sponsorship by top management, which helps choose a change-agent leader who can push the message and vision to management and the team to support a successful implementation.

Raed M. Skaf, PMP, PgMP, is director, project management office and budgeting, at Mobily, a telecom operator in Riyadh, Saudi Arabia.

Beyond Project Risks

To mitigate wider-ranging risks, organizations take an enterprise-wide approach.

Joel Crook, PMP, PgMP

From rockets to national nuclear security, my work has shown me that risk threatens far more than cost, scope and schedule. Wider-ranging risks—including to an organization's reputation, workers' safety, a country's security and the environment—permeate everything defense and aerospace organizations do, whether strategic or tactical. To proactively manage risk, organizations in these and other fields are increasingly implementing enterprise risk management (ERM).

ERM is a risk-based approach to managing an organization in any industry, and it can be highly effective in supporting strategic planning, controlling risk exposure and achieving objectives. Managing risk at the organizational level is very different from managing it at the project level. Project risk management is concerned with risks that arise from the project's scope, but at the portfolio or enterprise level, it is virtually impossible to

separate risk considerations from most organizational activities. For this reason, ERM is designed to break through organizational silos. It analyzes all risk across the enterprise, including operational risk, governance and compliance risk, project and program risk, financial risk and others. Risk management at this level plays an essential role in strategic planning and the growth of the organization.

ERM requires aggregating risk so that an overall risk position can be determined for a project, a program, a facility, a process, a site or the entire enterprise. Without risk aggregation, it's difficult for stakeholders and decision-makers to make a good comparison of alternatives. Aggregating allows business leaders to compare, for example, complex combinations of opportunities, expressed in dollars, and associated threats, expressed in units of reputation and units of environmental impact.

NORMALIZING RISK

But what is the common denominator that allows a cost risk to be aggregated with an environmental risk? And how can one aggregate financially tangible risks with financially intangible risks, such as community relationships, reputation and environmental impact? The answer begins with the normalization of risk.

To normalize risk, one must view it in terms of its cost impact. For example, a loss in corporate reputation can affect contract performance incentives and future contracts. An environmental impact risk could cause a cessation of operations for a period of time, which would equate to a specific dollar impact to sales. Once risks have been normalized in this way, they can be summed to indicate an overall risk position.

One of the most important benefits of ERM is that it enables corporate-level, risk-based decision making (RBDM). RBDM provides decision-makers with a realistic picture of likely outcomes to their strategic initiatives by integrating risk into the cost-benefit analysis of all strategic investments.

RBDM is a powerful tool for determining the optimal mix of projects that best achieves the organization's strategic goals and objectives. RBDM is used to compare the value of the candidate projects, and the ones with the best cost-to-benefit, with the highest probability of success, are selected to be part of the annual portfolio of planned projects—a top-down process.

Once the project has been authorized, a project manager is selected, and the RBDM risk analysis becomes input to the project or program's risk management. At this point, the project risk is further refined, monitored and controlled, and escalated as necessary. Risk management now becomes part of a continuous bottom-up process.

When risk analysis is part of this process, it is important to understand that most issues are caused by a combination of events or scenarios, rather than a single causal factor. For example, the probability of one being involved in a car accident is relatively low, but will increase dramatically if the driver is drowsy and it is storming. Scenario analysis is a quantitative analysis technique that attempts to consider how many different, and often benign, risks can be combined to create catastrophic consequences. As NASA's (U.S. National Aeronautics and Space Administration) *Risk-Informed Decision Making Handbook* puts it, "Scenarios are used to identify ways in which a system or process in its current state can evolve to an undesirable state."

BLACK SWAN EVENTS

Another aspect of ERM is contingency planning, which is developed in anticipation of the realization of a risk. The contingency plan addresses low-probability, high-impact risks because of the severity of the impact these risks can pose.

The most unpredictable category of low-probability risk is "black swan" events. These events often result from the synergistic realization of multiple risks or natural disasters, and their consequence can be extreme. When a 15-meter tsunami hit the Fukushima nuclear power facility in 2011 following a major earthquake, it disabled three of the facility's reactors. All three reactor cores melted in the three days that followed. Although black swan events can't always be prevented, contingency planning will increase the probability of successfully managing the event, should it occur.

Contingency plans should identify all trigger events as well as potential amounts of time, money or other resources needed to handle known—or even sometimes unknown—threats and opportunities. The plan is executed if a predetermined trigger event occurs. Once a plan is in place, regular training and practice will enable effective corporate-level management of the organization when it is in crisis.

When ERM is integral to key decision-making processes, the probability of meeting enterprise-level business objectives and preparing the organization to manage future risks improves. But as powerful as ERM is, it is important to remember that it is not a crystal ball, and it can't be implemented overnight. ERM requires an investment of time and money, and the dedication of skilled and experienced leaders.

Joel Crook, PMP, PgMP, is the director of enterprise risk management for Consolidated Nuclear Security (CNS) LLC, Oak Ridge, Tennessee, USA. Before that, he was a program director for ATK Aerospace Systems, responsible for a system-level space launch vehicle program. The views are those of the author and do not necessarily reflect those of the United States government or any agency thereof, CNS or ATK.

A Richer Chorus

How organizations can use project management to increase diversity.

Colleen G. White, PMP

Diversity and inclusion are often viewed as "feel good" functions within HR departments, which provide programs and activities for employees who have time to attend. My organization, a Fortune 500 healthcare services company, views diversity and inclusion very differently—so much so that it includes a program manager in its efforts toward these goals.

Cardinal Health believes that an inclusive strategy that seeks diverse perspectives lets us better anticipate the needs of the marketplace and leverage the talent of our people as a competitive advantage. In other words, diversity and inclusion are business imperatives and are managed as such.

DIVERSITY GOALS AS PROJECTS

At Cardinal, a Diversity and Inclusion Council chaired by the CEO approves the overall diversity and inclusion strategy. Next, senior leaders collaborate with the diversity and inclusion team to develop goals that support the

strategy. These goals are executed as projects with defined scope, accountability, deliverables, milestones, risk
and metrics. In my role as program manager, I work with
project sponsors to ensure the projects are executed according to plan and are collectively providing defined
benefits. I also work with the project teams to ensure
scope is maintained, milestones are met and issues are resolved. Project updates are provided at a regular cadence,
and overall progress is measured by representation metrics and trended employee satisfaction scores. These are
reported annually to the Diversity and Inclusion Council.

THE CHALLENGES

Because it's so rare for project management practices to
be used in diversity and inclusion, we've run into several
challenges. The projects and programs we support can

take years to see measurable results. This can make adhering to timelines difficult, and robust project planning, scope control and stakeholder management are critical in managing the work.

Another difficulty has been reporting, as most stakeholders have no project management software and aren't familiar with project management terms such as requirements or scope creep. Working with our Operational Excellence department, I adapted reporting formats from its Lean Six Sigma toolkit. We chose a format with all key items on one page—business case, goals, scope, risk, stakeholders, deliverables and key milestones. This has made project tracking and reporting easier for all stakeholders.

OUTCOMES

One project that has been particularly rewarding for me is Engaging Men to Advance Women, which began in 2013. Its goal is to create an even more diverse and gender-balanced culture in which men are supporting the progress of women into leadership. Project participants are male leaders at the vice president level and above, trained to engage in the company's efforts to increase the number of women in leadership positions. Among the groups led by men participating in the project, female promotions as a percent of total promotions experienced a double-digit increase. Like all projects with a goal to change culture, this multiyear project requires much communication and stakeholder management.

Colleen G. White, PMP, is the director of human resources information systems at Cardinal Health in Dublin, Ohio, USA.